Cooking New Orleans Style!

Compiled by
The Women of All Saints' Episcopal Church
New Orleans, Louisiana

Copies of *Cooking New Orleans Style* may be obtained from:

La Bonne Cuisine
100 Rex Drive
New Orleans, Louisiana 70123
(504) 737-1416

Contents

Acknowledgements

Creative Writing
The Very Rev. William C. Morris

Cover Design
Craig Kraemer – Graphic Designer

Photographs
City Park Oak Trees – Eileen Mitchell
Pete Fountain – compliments of Pete Fountain Productions
Louisiana Swamp Exhibit – compliments of Audubon Park
Jax Brewery – compliments of Jax Brewery
Riverwalk – compliments of Rault Riverwalk, Inc.
French Quarter Festival – compliments of French Quarter Festival
French Quarter Grill Work – Eileen Mitchell
New Orleans Cemetery – Eileen Mitchell

NEW ORLEANS

New Orleans began as an Old World city in the New World—a carefully planned walled town established by the French government to secure control of the lower Mississippi. The French Quarter preserves the original layout, even though none of the original buildings has survived. The plan was very practical. The narrow streets were cool in the hot climate. The closeness of the houses kept everything within easy walking distance. The ramparts which originally ran around the city on all but the river side provided both defense against attack and internal control. Rampart Street's name preserves the memory of the old city wall, which decayed and was finally torn down.

In Old World fashion, commercial and residential space existed side by side, often in the same building. Outdoor space took the form of patios and courtyards, rather than lawns and gardens open to public view. Often, kitchens were separate buildings at the backs of the narrow lots. This arrangement protected the houses from heat, cooking odors, and spying servants. Dining rooms, servants' quarters, storage rooms, and bedrooms for the young men of the family might also be included in the kitchen buildings, which were sometimes larger than the main houses.

The humid climate was destructive, and fire was a constant danger. On Good Friday, in 1788, a large part of New Orelans burned down. Except for the Ursuline Convent, itself a replacement of the original, the buildings you see in the Quarter were built either by the Spanish or by Americans. New Orleans' famous ironwork, too, is either Spanish or American, rather than French. The elaborate, lacy cast-iron designs which many people find so striking were prefabricated and sold through catalogues to home-owners who wanted to update their houses, along with cast-iron fences, gates, chairs, benches, and tables.

New Orleans was already a city when it became American, in 1803, as part of the Louisiana Purchase. The citizens, who were not consulted, were not pleased with the change. They did not speak English, and their experience with Americans had not been a happy one. As more and more Americans came to New Orleans, they built a new city, upriver across Canal Street. The median on Canal Street is, to this day, called "the neutral ground", meaning a piece of land which belonged neither to the French nor to the Americans. The Americans did not copy New Orleans customs about houses. Instead, they built American-style houses surrounded by lawns and gardens. That is how "the Garden District" got its name. For a time, conflict was so intense that New Orleans was actually several municipalities, side by side.

By the beginning of the twentieth century, much of the French Quarter had become a slum. Now-famous writers just starting out lived there, not because it was charming, but because it was cheap. It was poverty, rather than tradition, which preserved the French Quarter for us to enjoy. Fortunately, by the 1930s, New Orleanians had begun to realize what a treasure it was, and made it one of the earliest protected historic districts in the country.

5

CREOLE AND CAJUN

Creole and *Cajun* are not the same, and neither is their cooking.

A *Creole* is someone of Old World ancestry and culture born in the New World. Creoles were, in a sense, orphans of colonization—people who were not Native Americans, but who had an indirect experience of the European culture which shaped them. They were frequently seen as 'hicks' by people born in Europe. To compensate, some of them were excessively 'proper' and paid close attention to European fashions.

Cajuns (the word is a corruption of "Acadian") are seen as different in Louisiana, even though they are technically Creoles, too. They are descended from the French who settled in the seventeenth century in the part of Canada known in French as Acadia and in English as Nova Scotia. Great Britain acquired Nova Scotia in 1713. However, the Acadians refused to adopt the English language, customs, or laws. After a generation of conflict, the British began in 1755 to deport them to other English colonies. The Cajuns, however, preferred the French background and Roman Catholic religion of Louisiana and were warmly welcomed by the Spanish governors, who gave them land and assistance, partly out of compassion and partly because Louisiana needed a larger population. A few Cajuns arrived as early as 1756 and settled West of New Orleans. Thousands more followed. Over 1500 arrived in 1786. They worked, as they had in Nova Scotia, as farmers, trappers, and fishermen.

Creoles copied the current fashions of Europe in cooking and culture. Cajuns, in contrast, maintained the language, customs, and cooking they had brought from France two centuries before. Creole cooking tends to be restrained and elegant. Cajun cooking is more robust. Often, the dishes are the same, and the difference is in the cooks.

THE AVENUE OF OAKS IN NEW ORLEANS' CITY PARK

Early plantation owners planted avenues of oaks like these as approaches to their houses.

APPETIZERS & BEVERAGES

Asparagus Roll-Ups

24 slices white sandwich bread, crusts removed
8 ounces cream cheese, softened
4 ounces blue cheese, crumbled
1 egg
Dash each Tabasco sauce, Worcestershire sauce, lemon juice
6 ounces canned bacon-flavored bits
24 asparagus spears, canned
¾ cup margarine, melted

Roll bread flat with a rolling pin. Set aside. In a small mixing bowl, combine cheeses, egg, Tabasco sauce, Worcestershire sauce and lemon juice until smooth. Spread mixture on each slice of bread. Sprinkle bacon-flavored bits over cheese mixture. Drain asparagus spears. Place one spear lengthwise on each slice of bread. Roll up like a jelly roll around spear. Pinch closed. Dip in melted butter and cut each roll into thirds. Place on ungreased cookie sheet. Bake for 15 minutes in a 400°F oven. Yield: 72 appetizers.
NOTE: May be frozen before baking.

Antipasto

1 bay leaf
1 sprig parsley
2 cloves garlic
1 rib celery, coarsely chopped
½ teaspoon oregano
1½ cups olive oil
1½ cups vinegar
2 teaspoons salt
½ teaspoon white pepper
1 8-ounce can mushrooms (fancy jumbo)

Place bay leaf, parsley, garlic, celery, and oregano into a cheesecloth spice bag. Bring oil, vinegar, salt and pepper to a boil. Drop in spice bag and simmer for 20 minutes. Drop in mushrooms and simmer 15 minutes longer. Remove spice bag and put remaining ingredients into a crock or jar to cool. Store in refrigerator at least 3 days before serving.
NOTE: Garbanzos, artichoke hearts and olives may also be prepared in the same manner, but should be done separately.

Mushrooms Stuffed with Crab Meat

1 cup crab meat
1 tablespoon Italian bread crumbs
1/2 teaspoon onion puree
1 tablespoon chopped parsley
1 tablespoon chopped chives
1 teaspoon lemon pepper
1 egg, lightly beaten
1 1/2 pounds large mushrooms
1/2 cup seasoned bread crumbs
2 tablespoons melted butter
Grated Parmesan cheese

Combine crab meat and bread crumbs. Add onion puree, parsley, chives and lemon pepper. Stir in egg. Trim stems from mushrooms and reserve for another use. Fill caps with mixture. Toss seasoned bread crumbs in melted butter then sprinkle on mushrooms. Top with Parmesan cheese. Bake at 350°F for 20 minutes. Serves 12-15.

Cheese Straws

15 ounces extra sharp cheddar cheese, grated
3/4 cup margarine
2 cups flour
1 1/4 teaspoons baking powder
1/2 teaspoon salt
4 or 5 drops Tabasco sauce
1/2 teaspoon cayenne pepper

Let cheese and margarine come to room temperature. Sift together flour, baking powder, and salt. Lightly blend in margarine and cheese. Add spices and flour, mix well. Put dough into cookie press and squeeze onto a lightly greased cookie sheet. Bake at 275°F for 10 to 15 minutes or until lightly browned. Cool. Store in airtight containers. These straws can be frozen.

Top cream cheese with pepper jelly as a cracker spread.

Hot Pepper Pecans

2 cups pecan halves
¼ cup butter or margarine, melted
4 teaspoons soy sauce
½ teaspoon Tabasco sauce

Spread pecans evenly in a 9×13×2 inch baking pan, then bake them at 300°F for 25 to 30 minutes or until lightly browned. Combine the remaining ingredients and mix well. Pour over the pecans and stir to coat all the pecans. Drain on paper towels. Store in airtight container.

Smoked Oyster Dip

1 8-ounce package cream cheese
1 3.6-ounce can smoked oysters
⅓ cup Pick-a-Pepper sauce
Chopped green onions to taste

Let cheese come to room temperature. Drain oysters and reserve oil. Mash oysters with a fork until finely minced. Blend together cream cheese, oysters, oil, Pick-a-Pepper sauce, and onion until smooth. Chill in refrigerator until mixture is firm. Serve with crackers of your choice.

Coffee

Coffee is special in New Orleans. It is always available, and never boiled. If it boils, it is thrown out as undrinkable. New Orleans coffee is dark-roasted, and is often mixed with an almost equal amount of chicory. A New Orleans saying describes it. It should be
"Black as the Devil,
Strong as Death,
Sweet as Love,
And hot as Hell."
Traditionally, people start the day with a cup of black coffee, and then have *cafe au lait* for breakfast, strong coffee mixed with an equal amount of hot milk.

Eggs will beat to a greater volume if at room temperature.

Iced Coffee

8 ounces instant coffee
1½ gallons very hot water
1½ gallons milk
16 ounces chocolate syrup
3 heaping tablespoons sugar
5 half gallons vanilla ice cream

In a large container, blend the coffee and the hot water. Let cool. Add milk, chocolate syrup and sugar. Pour into three gallon jars. When ready to serve, pour coffee mixture into a punch bowl, add large scoops of softened ice cream. Serve in punch cups.

Cafe Brulot

Thin slice of butter
12-14 cloves
Peelings of 2 oranges, cut in long curls
Peelings of 2 lemons, cut in long curls
8 heaping teaspoons dark brown sugar
10 ounces brandy
4 ounces triple sec
6 cinnamon sticks
Ground cinnamon
10 cups hot, strong coffee

In a large chafing dish, place butter, cloves, orange peel, lemon peel, brown sugar, brandy, triple sec, and cinnamon sticks over flame. Heat thoroughly and ignite. Agitate to keep flame burning. Slowly add pinches of ground cinnamon from above to flaming liquid. (Mixture will sparkle when cinnamon is added.) Pour in hot coffee. Serves 8-12 in demitasse cups. Be sure to dim lights for a dramatic effect.
NOTE: All ingredients must be hot in order to flame.

Christmas Egg Nog

6 quarts egg nog
1½ gallons skim milk
4 half-gallons vanilla ice cream
3 fifths bourbon
Ground nutmeg

In a large container, mix together the egg nog and milk. Add large scoops of ice cream. Blend in the whiskey. Sprinkle with nutmeg. Makes 3 gallons.

Soups & Gumbos

SECTION II

PETE FOUNTAIN AND HIS HALF FAST MARCHING CLUB

On Mardi Gras (Fat Tuesday) marching clubs like this famous one follow the Carnival parades, dispensing flowers and kisses to the women and stopping often for refreshments.

SOUPS & GUMBOS

MARDI GRAS

People call Mardi Gras "the Greatest Free Show on Earth"—but wait! That's not quite right. *Mardi Gras* is the name of the day before Ash Wednesday, when Lent begins. It means "Fat Tuesday." *Carnival* is the name of the celebration. It means "goodby to the meat," which, traditionally, wasn't eaten in Lent.

Carnival has two sides—parades and balls. Most balls are strictly formal and by invitation only—although a few of the newer Krewes (which is what Carnival organizations are called) throw public bashes. The balls start on Twelfth Night (the Epiphany, Jan. 6), and continue until Mardi Gras night. The parade season, on the other hand, is about 12 days long, ending on Mardi Gras. During this time, there are one or more parades every day or evening in New Orleans and in the surrounding communities. The parades are free to the spectators but not to the float riders, who have to pay for the whole thing, including the beads, doubloons, cups, and other trinkets thrown to the crowds. People scramble to catch these "treasures," and rate parades, not only on the basis of bands, costumes, and floats, but on how many "throws" they caught.

Crab and Corn Soup

6 ears fresh corn or 2½ cups frozen whole kernel corn
½ cup margarine
½ cup flour
½ cup minced green onions
1 quart chicken stock
1 quart half-and-half
1 tablespoon salt
1 teaspoon lemon pepper
Dash of Tabasco sauce
1 pound crabmeat, drained

Cut the kernels from the ears of corn and set aside. Discard the cobs. Melt the margarine in a heavy pot and blend in the flour to make a light roux. Add the green onions, cook until tender, stirring constantly. Blend in the chicken stock. Bring to a boil. Add the half-and-half and the corn. Season with salt, lemon pepper, and Tabasco sauce. Lower heat and simmer for about 20 minutes. Carefully fold in the crabmeat. Heat thoroughly and serve. Serves 6-8.

Oyster Artichoke Soup

2 dozen oysters
24 ounces quartered artichokes
2 cups strong chicken stock
1 cup chopped green onions
1 tablespoon chopped parsley
1 teaspoon thyme leaves
Salt and cayenne pepper to taste
½ cup melted butter
½ cup flour
2 cups cream

In a heavy saucepan, combine oysters, artichokes, chicken stock, onions, parsley, thyme, salt and pepper and bring to boil. Combine butter and flour for light roux. Stir into boiling soup. Stir in cream and simmer for 10 minutes. Serve with freshly chopped green onions and parsley for garnish. Serves 6-8.

Soups & Gumbos

Shrimp Artichoke Soup

8 ounces peeled raw shrimp, cut in halves
¼ cup margarine
6 green onions, finely chopped (green and white parts separated)
1 clove garlic, minced
2 tablespoons margarine
¼ cup flour
2 cups milk
3 cups chicken stock
1 pint half-and-half
1 14-ounce can artichoke hearts (reserve liquid)
1 tablespoon minced fresh parsley for garnish
salt and pepper to taste
1 tablespoon lemon juice

In a large skillet, saute shrimp, white parts of onions, and garlic in ¼ cup margarine for 15 minutes. Shrimp will be pink and onions tender. Remove shrimp and onions and reserve. Add 2 tablespoons margarine to drippings. Add flour and cook, stirring constantly, for 5 minutes. Slowly add 2 cups milk, stirring constantly (preferably with a whisk) until smooth and thickened to form a white sauce. Add the white sauce to the 3 cups of chicken stock in a large saucepan. Stir well. Add half-and-half, green part of onions, artichoke hearts cut in eighths, and the artichoke liquid. Simmer 20 minutes. Add shrimp, salt, and pepper. Simmer 10 minutes. Add lemon juice. Serve with parsley for garnish. Serves 6-8.

Gumbo

Gumbo is the sweet mystery of Louisiana cooking. It expresses the versatility, the frugality, and the multi-ethnic character of the state's cuisine. It can be elegant or homey, delicate or robust, very special, or a way of using leftovers. The traditional thickening for gumbo, filé (pronounced FEE-lay), made from powdered leaves of the sassafras tree, was contributed by the Indians, as was the custom of serving it with rice. Okra, the alternative thickening, came from Africa. The roux which forms the base of all but the fast-day gumbo z'herbes comes from France. The peppers which give it bite were contributed by the Spanish, who got them from the Indians of Central America. The result is something unique—dark, richly-seasoned, and full of good things, an appetizer, or a meal in itself.

Filé will make the gumbo stringy if it is heated after the filé has been added. One solution is to let people add the filé themselves at the table, so that the leftover gumbo can be reheated later.

Okra, the alternative thickening, can be added as the gumbo cooks. However, if you are using an iron pot, the gumbo will turn black. It tastes fine, and it won't hurt you, but some cooks don't like the color.

White rice is traditionally served with the gumbo, each person spooning as much into his bowl as he wants.

Chicken Andouille Gumbo

1 cup oil
2 pounds boned chicken meat (without skin), cut into bite-sized pieces
Cayenne pepper
1½ pounds andouille sausage cut into bite-sized pieces
1 cup flour
4 cups chopped onion
2 cups chopped celery
2 cups chopped bell pepper
1 tablespoon chopped garlic
8 cups stock*
Salt
Cayenne pepper
1 cup chopped green onions
1 cup chopped parsley
filé
cooked rice

Sprinkle chicken with cayenne pepper; brown in oil over medium heat in a Dutch oven. Add sausage and saute with chicken. Remove both from the pot. Remove from heat and strain fat. To make roux, over low heat, add flour to hot fat gradually, stirring all the while with a whisk. Over low heat, brown the roux, stirring constantly, until it turns a nutty brown color. Add onions, celery, bell pepper and garlic. Continue cooking over low heat until vegetables are tender, stirring constantly. Gradually add the stock; mix well. Add the chicken and sausage and bring to a boil. Reduce to simmer and cook for an hour or more. Season to taste. Approximately 10 minutes before serving, add green onions and parsley. Gumbo may or may not be served over rice. Two to three drops of sherry may be added to each serving or ¼ to ½ teaspoon of filé per serving may be added at the table as a flavor option. Makes 10-15 servings.

NOTES: Filé is a fine green powder of young, dried, ground sassafras leaves used in gumbo for flavor and thickening. For seafood gumbo, use seafood stock or equivalent and substitute fresh seafood for chicken and andouille.

*Chicken stock may be made with 2 16-ounce cans of stock plus 4 cups water or bouillon.

Hearty Seafood Gumbo

4 tablespoons oil
4 tablespoons flour
1 medium onion, chopped
½ cup chopped celery
½ cup chopped bell pepper
2 tablespoons chopped parsley
3 or 4 slices bacon
½ cup ham chunks
3 cloves garlic, crushed
1 pound okra (fresh or frozen) cut in ½ inch slices
32 ounces canned stewed tomatoes
1 cup crab meat
2 dozen large peeled shrimp
hot water
salt to taste
2 bay leaves
sprinkle of thyme
sprinkle of black pepper
¼ teaspoon Tabasco sauce

In a large pot, heat four tablespoons of oil. When well heated, sprinkle and stir in four level tablespoons of flour. Cook, stirring constantly, until brown but not burned. Add the onion, celery, bell pepper, and parsley. Simmer for 10 minutes, stirring often. Chop bacon and add to the pot with the ham chunks. Cook another five minutes. Add the garlic and okra. Simmer, stir and lift, until the okra stops being stringy, about 10 to 15 minutes. Add the tomatoes, a little at a time, over high heat. Add the crab meat and shrimp. Pour in some hot water, just enough to cover the mixture, and ½ teaspoon salt. Simmer 15 minutes with the cover on. Add more salt if desired. Add bay leaves, thyme, and black pepper. Cook 20 minutes more and add more water if gumbo is too thick. Serve with rice. Serves 6-8.

Microwaved Turkey Gumbo

1 turkey carcass
2 turkey legs or thighs
½ cup flour
¼ cup cooking oil
¼ cup bacon grease
4 ribs celery, chopped
2 medium onions, chopped
½ bell pepper, chopped
1 clove garlic, minced
¼ cup chopped parsley
½ pound okra, sliced
½ cup sliced smoked sausage
¼ cup Worcestershire sauce
Tabasco sauce to taste
¾ cup canned tomatoes
¾ tablespoon salt
2 slices bacon, cut in 1-inch pieces
1 bay leaf
Cayenne pepper to taste
½ teaspoon brown sugar
½ tablespoon lemon juice
2 cups rice, cooked

Crack the turkey carcass into pieces and place it and the legs in a deep 4-quart casserole, add 1 quart of water. Cover and microwave on high until it starts to boil. Reduce power to 30% and boil for 10 minutes. Remove the carcass and legs and cool. Remove the meat from the bones and discard the bones. Reserve the stock and meat. This all may be done beforehand and refrigerated overnight or frozen until a later date.

First, make the roux:
Combine the flour, oil, and bacon grease in a microwaveable 1-quart measure or mixing bowl. Microwave on high for 6 minutes, or until dark golden brown. Stir when there are 4 minutes remaining, when 2 minutes remain, when 1 minute remains, when 30 seconds remain, and at the end of this cooking period. If the roux is not dark enough, microwave another 30 seconds. Add the celery, onion, bell pepper, garlic, and parsley and mix well. Microwave on high for 4 to 5 minutes more, until vegetables are soft, but not brown. (You can make the roux this way, then use the traditional stove-top, longer-cooking method of making gumbo instead of continuing with the microwave method.)

In the 4-quart casserole, combine the roux with the okra and sausage and cook on high for 2 minutes. Add turkey stock and enough water to make 2 quarts. Mix in remaining ingredients, except brown sugar and lemon juice. Cover and continue cooking at 50% power for 30 to 35 minutes. Stir in brown sugar and lemon juice; let sit for a few minutes. Serve in heated bowls over rice, with a salad and French bread. Serves 8-10.

Seafood Sausage Gumbo

2 1-pound bags sliced, frozen okra (do not thaw)
2-4 tablespoons oil
4 tablespoons flour
4 tablespoons bacon grease
2 large onions, chopped
2 ribs celery, chopped
1 bell pepper, chopped
3 cloves garlic, chopped
1 pound turkey sausage
1 14½ ounce can stewed tomatoes
1 quart shrimp stock
2 quarts chicken stock
2 bay leaves
2 teaspoons liquid crab boil
1 teaspoon liquid smoke
1 teaspoon thyme
2 teaspoons salt
1 teaspoon pepper
2 cups crab meat
1 pound catfish fillets cut in bite-sized pieces
1½ pounds peeled shrimp

In a large, non-stick skillet fry okra in 2-4 tablespoons of oil until slimy consistency is gone (about 35-45 minutes). Stir okra frequently to keep from sticking. In another skillet put bacon grease and flour. Stir over medium heat until roux turns the color of peanut butter. To the roux add onions, celery, green pepper and garlic. Saute until vegetables are transparent. Cut turkey sausage in ¼ inch rounds, then in half, and add to roux and vegetables. Transfer the roux mixture and okra to a 8-10 quart pot. Add tomatoes, stock, bay leaves, crab boil, liquid smoke, thyme, salt and pepper. Add crab meat and catfish pieces. Simmer 20 minutes over medium heat, stirring frequently to keep from sticking. Add shrimp and cook 10 minutes more. If gumbo is too thick, add canned chicken broth or water to thin. This gumbo is best when prepared one day ahead and refrigerated. It will thicken as it chills. Heat it before adding additional liquid. Serve over rice. Makes a Cajun pot-full, but it freezes well. To make seafood stock: Place shrimp shells, onion (coarsely chopped), celery, and garlic into a pot. Add 2 quarts of water. Boil until liquid is reduced by half. Strain. Discard shells, etc. Season stock to taste.

Breads & Salads

THE FRENCH QUARTER FESTIVAL

Every April, this festival offers three fun-filled days for people of all ages and interests throughout the Vieux Carré (which is the French name of the French Quarter). It includes outdoor concerts, a huge jazz brunch, a battle of jazz bands, and other delights.

BREADS & SALADS

Good bread is a New Orleans staple and is served at every meal. In the European tradition, most people buy it fresh from the bakery instead of making it at home.

New Orleans French Bread

1 package dry yeast
1 tablespoon salt
1 tablespoon sugar
2 cups warm water
5-5½ cups flour
2 tablespoons butter, melted
2 tablespoons cornmeal

In a large bowl, dissolve the yeast, salt, and sugar in the warm water. Gradually stir in the flour, adding only until the mixture refuses to absorb more. On a floured board, knead the dough for 3 to 4 minutes. Transfer the dough to a greased bowl and brush the top lightly with butter. Cover with a damp cloth. Set the dough aside in a warm place to rise for 1½ hours, or until it is double in bulk. Butter a baking sheet and sprinkle it with cornmeal, shaking off the excess. Punch down the dough. Transfer the dough to a floured board and divide it into thirds. Roll each portion into an 8×13 inch rectangle. Roll each rectangle up from the long side, seal, and shape ends. Place the loaves on the prepared baking sheet and with a sharp knife, make several diagonal cuts across the tops. Brush lightly with melted butter. Let rise in a warm place about 45 minutes. Place the bread on the middle rack in the oven. Place a pan of hot water on the bottom of the oven. Bake at 450°F for 5 minutes. REDUCE OVEN TEMPERATURE to 350°F and continue baking for 30 minutes. Makes 3 loaves.

Pain Perdu (French Toast)

1 loaf (18-20 inches) dry French bread
3 eggs
½ cup milk
3 tablespoons butter
Confectioners sugar
Nutmeg

Carefully slice bread into ¾ inch slices. If bread is not really dry, place on baking sheet in 250°F oven until dry. Do not toast. Mix eggs and milk in a shallow, flat dish. Do not beat until frothy. Dip bread slices and turn to coat both sides. Set aside on plate for 3 to 5 minutes while melting 1 tablespoon butter in non-stick skillet. Heat to medium high and fry as many slices as will cover the skillet bottom. Turn when light brown, adding butter if necessary. Move the slices while cooking and adjust heat in order to brown evenly. Continue until all bread is fried. Serve hot with sprinkled nutmeg and sifted confectioners sugar. Serves 4-6.

Beignets

(French Market Doughnuts)

½ cup boiling water
2 tablespoons shortening
¼ cup sugar
½ teaspoon salt
½ cup evaporated milk
½ package dry yeast
¼ cup warm water
1 egg, beaten
3¾ cups sifted flour
Confectioners' sugar

In a large mixing bowl, pour the boiling water over the shortening, sugar, and salt. Add the milk and let stand until warm. In a small bowl, dissolve the yeast in the warm water and add to the milk mixture with the egg. Stir in 2 cups flour and beat. Add enough flour to make a soft dough. Place the dough in a greased bowl, turning to grease the top. Cover with waxed paper and a cloth and chill until ready to use. On a lightly floured surface, roll the dough to ⅛ inch thickness. Do not let dough rise before frying. Cut into 2-inch squares and fry, a few at a time, in deep, hot fat (360°F). Brown on 1 side, turn and brown on the other side. Drain on paper towels. Sprinkle with the confectioners' sugar and serve hot. Makes 30 doughnuts.

King Cake

Christmas in New Orleans lasts for twelve days. The Feast of the Epiphany, which celebrates the arrival of the Wise Men, simultaneously concludes Christmas and begins the Carnival Season. On that day, and on almost every day thereafter until Lent begins, New Orleanians devour thousands of King cakes — circles of dough, decorated with purple, gold, and green sugar or frosting, each containing a bean or a plastic baby. At a party, whoever gets the slice of cake containing the bean or the baby is king or queen for the week, and must provide the King cake for the next party.

King cakes range from simple (decorated sweet dough) to sublime (pastry filled with cheese or cooked fruit). Once a special dessert for Epiphany, they are now eaten from Epiphany (January 6) through Mardi Gras (Fat Tuesday), the day before Lent begins. On Ash Wednesday, rich dishes and sweet desserts disappear from the table until Easter.

Many New Orleans bakeries now ship King cakes to New Orleanians living away, or to people who have visited New Orleans and enjoyed one.

King Cake

DOUGH:
3½ cups flour, sifted
¼ cup sugar
1 package active dry yeast
1 teaspoon salt
½ cup water
½ cup milk
¼ cup butter
1 egg
FILLING:
1¼ cups brown sugar
2 teaspoons cinnamon
⅓ cup butter, softened
ICING:
1 cup confectioners sugar
1 teaspoon vanilla
2 tablespoons milk
1 teaspoon oil

In a large mixing bowl, mix 1 cup flour, sugar, yeast and salt. Place water, milk, and butter in saucepan over low heat and heat until liquids are warm and butter is melted. Gradually add liquid to dry ingredients and beat with an electric mixer for 2 minutes at medium speed. Add egg and 1 cup flour, or enough to make a thick batter. Beat at high speed for 2 minutes. Gradually add enough of the remaining flour to make a stiff dough.

Turn out onto a heavily floured board and knead 5 to 10 minutes or until dough is smooth. Add flour to board as needed to prevent dough from sticking. Place ball of dough into greasesd bowl; turn once to bring greased side up. Cover with a damp cloth and let rise in a warm place until double in bulk (about 1½ hours).

Punch down, turn out onto a lightly floured board. Knead about 5 times. Divide dough in half. Roll half of the dough into a 25×15 inch oblong. Spread with 2 tablespoons softened butter. Sprinkle with half of the brown sugar and cinnamon mixture. Roll tightly, starting with wide side. Pinch the edges.

Repeat this procedure with rest of dough. Twist the two rolls and attach ends. Place ring on greased baking sheet. Cover with greased waxed paper and towel. Let rise in warm place for 1½ hours or until doubled. Place in a preheated 375° oven; bake for 20 to 25 minutes until golden. After cake has cooled, spread icing on top. Decorate with gold, purple and green sugars. Serves 12.

Icing: Combine sugar, vanilla, and milk. Beat for about 1 minute with electric mixer. Add oil and beat until creamy. If icing is too thick, add a few drops of milk, beat well.

Breads & Salads

Buttermilk Biscuits

2 cups flour
4 teaspoons baking powder
1/2 teaspoon salt
1/2 teaspoon cream of tartar
2 teaspoons sugar
1/2 cup shortening
2/3 cup buttermilk*

In a bowl, sift together the flour, baking powder, salt, cream of tartar and sugar. Add the shortening and cut it into the dry mixture until the mixture resembles coarse crumbs. With a fork, stir in the milk and continue stirring, until the dough follows the fork around the bowl.

Transfer the mixture to a floured surface and knead it for 30 seconds. Pat the dough out to a 1/2 inch thickness. Using a biscuit cutter, cut into 16 biscuits. Bake the biscuits on an ungreased cookie sheet in a 400°F preheated oven for 10 to 12 minutes, until golden brown.

*If you do not have buttermilk, use 1 tablespoon vinegar or lemon juice PLUS enough whole milk to make 1 cup. Stir. Let sit for a few minutes. Use in place of buttermilk.

Raised Biscuits

2 1/2 cups flour
1/2 teaspoon soda
1/2 teaspoon salt
3-4 tablespoons sugar
6 tablespoons shortening
1 package yeast
1 cup buttermilk
Butter

Sift dry ingredients. Blend in shortening. Dissolve yeast in warmed buttermilk. Combine dry ingredients and buttermilk, mixing quickly. Turn out onto a floured surface and knead 20-30 strokes. Roll out dough to 1/4 to 1/2 inch thick and cut with a cookie cutter. Place one biscuit on top of the first after dipping the top biscuit in butter. Let rise until double. Bake 12-15 minutes at 375°F.

Cornmeal Biscuits

1½ cups unsifted flour
½ cup cornmeal
3 teaspoons baking powder
1 tablespoon sugar (optional)
¼ teaspoon salt
¼ cup butter or margarine
½ cup milk

Combine flour, cornmeal, baking powder, sugar and salt in a bowl. Cut in butter or margarine until mixture resembles coarse cornmeal. Stir in milk. Dough will be stiff. Turn out on a lightly-floured surface and roll or pat out to ½ inch thickness. Cut out with 2 inch round cutter and place on a lightly greased cookie sheet. Bake in a preheated 450°F oven for about 12 minutes — or until lightly browned.

Buttermilk Griddle Cakes

2 cups flour
¼ cup sugar
1 teaspoon baking soda
1 teaspoon salt
2 tablespoons cornmeal
1 cup buttermilk
1½ cups milk
1 egg
1 tablespoon oil

Into a large mixing bowl sift together the flour, sugar, baking soda, and salt. Add the cornmeal. In another mixing bowl combine the buttermilk, milk, egg, and oil. Add the liquid mixture to the dry ingredients and stir just enough to moisten the dry ingredients. Do not beat. Heat a griddle or skillet and grease if necessary. Drop the batter onto the hot griddle by spoonfuls. The cakes are ready to turn when air bubbles form on the surface of the cake. Turn them only once. Serve hot with melted butter and syrup. Serves 3-6.

To proof yeast combine 1 teaspoon sugar with the yeast and warm water called for in the recipe. If the mixture bubbles up quickly, the yeast is good.

Breads & Salads

Easter Bread

2 packages yeast
¼ cup warm water
1 cup sugar
1 cup light cream or milk, scalded and cooled
½ cup melted butter
1 teaspoon salt
3 eggs, well beaten
2 teaspoons ground cardamon
2 teaspoons grated lemon peel
2 tablespoons grated orange peel
1 cup golden raisins
1 cup sliced almonds (optional)
6 to 7 cups flour (2 cups of this can be rye flour)

In a large bowl dissolve yeast in warm water. Add sugar, milk, butter and salt. Beat in eggs, spices, peels, raisins, and nuts; beat well until thoroughly combined. Gradually add 5 cups flour, one cup at a time. Blend until smooth. Flour a board or countertop heavily with part of the remaining flour. Turn soft dough out onto board and sprinkle with more flour. Knead until very smooth, about 12-20 minutes, adding flour as needed. Place dough in a large buttered bowl. Turn dough to coat on all sides with butter. Keep covered in a warm place and let rise until doubled in bulk, about 2 hours. Punch down dough. Form dough into two round loaves. Place on two greased cookie sheets, cover with a cloth, and let rise until almost doubled in bulk. Bake in moderate oven, 350°F, for 20 minutes or until golden brown. Serve hot or cool. This bread freezes well when wrapped airtight.

Zucchini Bread

3 eggs
1 cup oil
2 cups sugar
2 cups grated zucchini
2 teaspoons vanilla
3 cups flour, sifted
1 teaspoon baking soda
¼ teaspoon baking powder
1 teaspoon salt
3 teaspoons cinnamon
½ cup nuts

In the bowl of an electric mixer beat the eggs until light and creamy. Add the oil, sugar, zucchini, and vanilla and mix lightly, but well. In a separate bowl mix the flour, baking soda, baking powder, salt, and cinnamon. Add the dry ingredients to the liquid mixture with the nuts and blend well. Pour the batter into 2 well-greased and floured 9"×5"×3" loaf pans. Bake at 325°F for 1 hour. Remove the loaves from the pans and transfer them to wire racks to cool. Makes 2 loaves.

Crescent Rolls

2 packages dry yeast
½ cup warm water
½ cup milk
½ cup sugar
½ cup shortening
2 teaspoons salt
4½-5 cups flour
3 eggs
½ cup melted butter

In a small bowl soften the yeast in the water. In a saucepan bring the milk to a boil and add the sugar, shortening, and salt. Transfer the mixture to a large bowl and cool to lukewarm. Stir 1½ cups of the flour into the milk mixture and beat well. Add the yeast and eggs. Beat thoroughly until smooth. Stir in enough of the remaining flour to make a moderately stiff dough. Transfer the dough to a lightly floured surface and knead 5 to 8 minutes until smooth and elastic. Shape the dough into a ball. Place in a lightly greased bowl and turn once. Cover and let rise in a warm place until double in bulk, about 1 to 1½ hours.

Punch the dough down and transfer it to a lightly floured surface. Cover and let rest 10 minutes. Divide the dough into 3 balls. Roll each ball into a 12-inch circle. Brush the dough with the melted butter. Cut into 12 pie-shaped wedges. To shape crescents, begin at the wide end of the wedge and roll toward the point. Place the rolls point side down on greased baking sheets about 2-3 inches apart. Cover the rolls with plastic wrap or a damp cloth and let rise in a warm place until double in bulk, about 30 to 45 minutes. Brush the rolls with melted butter. Bake at 400°F for 10 to 12 minutes. Makes 36 rolls.

Breads & Salads

Hearty Wheat Bread

2 cups warm water (80° to 95° F)
2 packages yeast
½ cup peanut oil
2 teaspoons salt
½ cup honey
½ cup wheat or oat bran
2 tablespoons wheat germ
3 cups whole wheat flour
3 cups bread flour

Pour water into a bowl, add yeast and stir to dissolve. Add oil, salt, honey and blend well. Stir in bran, wheat germ and whole wheat flour, a cup at a time, and beat until dough is smooth. Add bread flour in a similar manner until dough is stiff. Turn dough out onto a heavily floured board. Knead dough, adding flour as needed, until dough is no longer sticky. Kneading is complete when dough is smooth and satiny. Let dough rise until double (about 1½ hours at 80°F). Punch dough down, divide into two equal loaves and place into greased bread pans. Allow to rise until almost doubled (45 minutes to 1½ hours). Bake in center of oven at 350°F for 40 minutes or until crust is nicely browned. Remove from pans and cool on a rack.

Orange Pumpkin Bread

2½ cups flour
2 cups sugar
1½ teaspoons baking soda
1¼ teaspoons salt
¾ teaspoon cinnamon
¾ teaspoon ground nutmeg
¾ cup peanut oil or vegetable oil
¾ cup orange juice
3 eggs
4 tablespoons grated orange peel
1 16-ounce can pumpkin
½ to ¾ cup raisins
¾ to 1 cup chopped walnuts or pecans

In a large mixing bowl combine flour, sugar, soda, salt, cinnamon and nutmeg. Mix well and then add the next five ingredients. Beat with a wooden spoon or use a slow speed on the mixer. Fold in nuts and raisins and blend well. Pour batter into 2 greased loaf pans. Bake in a preheated 350° oven for 1 hour or until a toothpick inserted near the center comes out clean.
NOTE: This is nice for presents at holiday time when it is baked in miniature loaf pans.

Rice Salad

3 cups cooled, cooked rice
½ cup chopped onion
½ cup chopped sweet pickle
1 teaspoon salt
¼ teaspoon pepper
1 cup mayonnaise
1 teaspoon prepared mustard
¼ cup diced pimento
4 hard boiled eggs, chopped

Blend all ingredients. Chill. Serves 6-8.

Bean Salad

4 cans of your choice of beans (red kidney, garbanzo, black, pinto, white, cut green, etc.)
1 cup chopped onions
Celery seeds to taste
2 minced cloves garlic
½ cup chopped celery
1 teaspoon dry mustard
3 tablespoons wine vinegar
¼ cup olive oil
Salt and pepper

Rinse, drain and combine beans. Add remaining ingredients, mix well, and season with salt and pepper if desired. Chill overnight.

Honey Mustard Dressing

½ cup honey
¼ cup Dijon mustard
¼ teaspoon cayenne pepper
1 teaspoon lemon juice
¼ teaspoon Worcestershire sauce
½ cup heavy cream

Mix honey, mustard, pepper, lemon juice and Worcestershire sauce. Reduce heavy cream over medium-high heat, stirring constantly, until thickened. Stir into other ingredients. Chill.

Sweet and Sour 5 Bean Salad

1 16-ounce can green beans
1 8-ounce can small lima beans
1 16-ounce can yellow wax beans
1 16-ounce can Italian beans
1 15-ounce can red beans
8-ounce jar black olives
8-ounce jar green olives
1 medium red onion, sliced thin
½ pound mushrooms, sliced
1 bell pepper, sliced thin
½ cup pimento
¾ cup sugar
⅓ cup salad oil
⅔ cup cider vinegar
1 teaspoon salt
1 teaspoon garlic salt

Drain the beans and olives and place in a large mixing bowl. Gently fold in the onion, mushrooms, bell pepper, and pimento. In a saucepan mix the sugar, oil, vinegar, salt and garlic salt. Bring to a boil. Cook dressing until sugar is dissolved and pour over mixed beans. Chill thoroughly. Serves 10.
NOTE: Must be prepared at least one day in advance and can be held in refrigerator for five days. The longer it sits, the better it gets.

Broccoli Vinaigrette

2 slices bacon, cooked crisp
1 bunch fresh broccoli
6 green onions, chopped
2 hard boiled eggs, chopped
4 tablespoons wine vinegar
½-1 teaspoon sugar
Salt and pepper to taste

Fry bacon until crisp; reserve drippings. Crumble bacon. Wash broccoli and break into bite-sized pieces. Stems may be used if peeled and sliced. Add green onions, eggs, and crumbled bacon. Heat vinegar and sugar till dissolved. Pour hot bacon drippings and heated vinegar over broccoli mixture and toss. Add salt and pepper if desired. Serve immediately or at room temperature. Do not make ahead of time.

Chicken and Mango Salad

DRESSING (Make several hours or the night before):

1 green onion

1 tablespoon Dijon mustard*

¼ teaspoon white pepper

1 orange, peeled and cut in sections

⅜ cup white vinegar

½ cup orange juice

1 cup vegetable oil

2 teaspoons freshly grated ginger root

In a blender puree the green onion, mustard, pepper and orange sections. Add vinegar and orange juice. Add salt to taste if desired. Slowly add the oil and continue beating until it thickens. Stir in ginger root.
*Use Creole mustard for a delightful change of flavor.

SALAD:

8 chicken breast halves

2 red bell peppers, cut in fine strips

2 avocados

4 mangoes

2 heads of Bibb lettuce*

2 tablespoons soy sauce

Boil chicken breasts in salted water. Onions and a bit of lemon juice in the water will add flavor to the chicken. Cut the chicken in thin strips. Peel and slice the avocados and mangoes. Arrange the lettuce on individual plates. Top with chicken strips, avocados, mangoes and red bell peppers. Drizzle soy sauce over these ingredients. Pour dressing over all, top with toasted sesame seeds if desired, and serve. Serves 6.
*1 head of Boston lettuce may be substituted.

Tomatoes Vinaigrette

2 one-pound cans peeled whole tomatoes

2 tablespoons vinegar

1½ teaspoons sugar

Salt and pepper to taste

½ teaspoon dill weed

1 medium-sized white onion

Empty cans of tomatoes into a dish. Carefully lift out tomatoes and place them into a serving dish. Combine vinegar and sugar and spoon over tomatoes. Season to taste with salt and pepper. Sprinkle with dill. Slice onion into thin slices, separate rings and arrange over tomatoes. Cover and chill. This is a good salad for winter when good fresh tomatoes are hard to find.

Breads & Salads

Seven Layer Salad

Iceberg lettuce, torn into bite-sized pieces
Italian herbs, sprinkled over lettuce
Green and red bell peppers, seeded and finely chopped
Celery, chopped
Onions, finely chopped
1 8-ounce can water chestnuts, finely chopped
Raw frozen green peas, thawed
1 or 2 cups mayonnaise or mayonnaise-type spread
2 or 3 teaspoons sugar
Parmesan cheese, grated
Tomatoes, sliced or quartered
Bacon, cooked crisp and crumbled
Hard-boiled eggs

Quantities of above ingredients depend upon size of bowl and your own taste. Arrange first seven ingredients in layers in a glass bowl in order given. Cover with a layer of mayonnaise. Sprinkle with sugar and a generous amount of Parmesan cheese. Cover and let it stand in refrigerator all day or overnight. Garnish with crumbled bacon, tomatoes and sliced hard-boiled eggs.

Cranberry Salad

2 cups cranberries
1 orange, peel included
1 cup pecans
2 cups sugar
2 tablespoons unflavored gelatin
½ cup cold water
1½ cups boiling water

Slice orange and remove seeds. Grind orange and cranberries in a blender or food processor. Chop nuts. Mix fruit and nuts in a bowl; mix in sugar, cover and allow to sit for 1½ hours. Soften gelatin in ½ cup cold water. Dissolve in 1½ cups boiling water. Add gelatin to fruit mixture and mix well. Pour into molds or a 7×12 inch pan and refrigerate until firm. Serve on a bed of lettuce. 10-12 servings.

THE JAX BREWERY

When the brewery closed, it was remodeled into a handsome shopping mall, offering a variety of shops and eating-places.

VEGETABLES

Lemon Broccoli Amandine

2 pounds fresh broccoli
½ cup slivered almonds
1 tablespoon butter
⅓ cup milk
2 tablespoons lemon juice
¼ teaspoon lemon pepper
6 ounces cream cheese, softened

Separate broccoli into flowerets. Peel and cut stems into bite-sized pieces. Cook broccoli until slightly tender. Saute almonds in butter until golden brown. Combine remaining ingredients in saucepan over medium heat, stirring until smooth. Pour over broccoli. Sprinkle with almonds.

Cauliflower au Gratin

1 medium head cauliflower
1 cup sour cream
1 cup grated sharp cheese
2 teaspoons toasted sesame seeds
salt and pepper to taste

Separate cauliflower into flowerets. Cook in boiling salted water until tender; drain well. Place half the flowerets in a one-quart casserole. Season with salt and pepper. Spread with ½ cup of sour cream and ½ cup cheese. Top with 1 teaspoon sesame seeds. Repeat with remaining cauliflower, sour cream and cheese. Top with remaining sesame seeds. Bake uncovered at 350°F until cheese melts and casserole is heated through, about 10 minutes.

Cauliflower au Beurre Noir

1 medium head cauliflower
3 tablespoons butter
1 cup fine dry bread crumbs
1 cup grated cheddar cheese

Remove outer leaves and stalks from a head of cauliflower. Separate into flowerets. Cook in boiling salted water for 10 minutes. Drain and set aside. In a medium skillet, melt butter and stir in breadcrumbs until lightly browned. Melt one-half cup grated cheese in browned crumbs. Combine with cauliflower. Serves 4.

Vegetables

Green Bean and Artichoke Casserole (Microwave)

3 16-ounce cans French style green beans
1 16-ounce can artichoke quarters (cut in half)
1¼ cup seasoned bread crumbs (divided)
1 cup freshly grated Parmesan cheese
1 teaspoon garlic powder
3 tablespoons olive oil
1½ cups reserved liquid from beans and artichokes
¼ teaspoon Tabasco sauce
2 tablespoons butter

Drain beans and artichokes. Reserve 1½ cups liquid. Place beans and artichokes in 3-quart casserole. Add 1 cup bread crumbs, grated cheese, garlic powder, olive oil, Tabasco sauce, and 1½ cups of reserved liquid from beans and artichokes. Mix well. Microwave for 5 minutes at full power. Remove from microwave and mix well to distribute cheese. Then add remaining ¼ cup crumbs over the top of the casserole. Dot with butter. Microwave for additional 1-2 minutes to melt butter.

Green Beans Amandine

1 2½-ounce package slivered almonds
13 slices bacon
1 large onion, chopped
½ cup sugar
½ cup vinegar
1 20-ounce package frozen French style green beans

Place almonds in a single layer in pan. Brown in a 350°F oven about 10 minutes, stirring occasionally. Fry bacon until crisp. Drain on paper towels. Crumble. In a large skillet, sauté onions in a small amount of bacon grease until transparent. Add sugar and vinegar. Cook until slightly thickened. Add partially thawed green beans to sauce. Mix thoroughly. Layer beans and almonds in 9×13 inch dish. Bake at 350°F for 20 minutes. Top with crumbled bacon. Bake 10 minutes more. Serves 6.

Burgundy Onion Rings

6 large onions
¼ cup butter
2 whole cloves
½ teaspoon garlic salt
¼ teaspoon pepper
1 cup Burgundy wine

Cut onions into ¼ inch slices and separate them into rings. Melt butter in a large skillet, add the onions and cook them, stirring until they are well coated. Add cloves, salt and pepper and sauté onions until golden. Add the wine, cover and simmer for about 15 minutes. Discard the cloves. Remove the cover and cook onions until liquid is reduced almost to a glaze. Serves 4.

Cajun Bar-B-Que Beans

1 pound ground meat
1 medium onion, chopped
1 medium bell pepper, chopped
1 31-ounce can pork and beans
6 tablespoons catsup
4 tablespoons Worcestershire sauce
¼ cup packed dark brown sugar
½ cup barbecue sauce
Dash of Tabasco sauce

Brown the meat in a large skillet. Pour off the grease. Stir in the onion and bell peppers and sauté slightly. Transfer the ground meat, onion, and bell pepper into a 2-quart casserole. Add remaining ingredients. Mix well. Bake at 350°F for 45 minutes.

Orange Glazed Carrots

2 pounds small whole carrots
½ cup orange juice
½ cup sugar
1 tablespoon cornstarch
1 teaspoon salt
1 tablespoon grated orange rind
2 tablespoons butter

Wash carrots, scrape and cut in half diagonally. Parboil 15 minutes. Place carrots in a buttered casserole dish. Combine remaining ingredients in saucepan and heat until cornstarch is dissolved and sauce is slightly thickened. Pour over carrots. Dot with butter. Bake 20 minutes. Uncover and bake a few minutes longer until some of the liquid has evaporated. Serves 6.

Vegetables

Creole Eggplant Casserole

2 large or 3 medium eggplants
1 cup water
½ teaspoon salt
1 cup each chopped onion, bell pepper, and celery
3 tablespoons oil
4 ounces seasoned breadcrumbs (reserve 2 tablespoons)
2 eggs, slightly beaten
6 ounces cheddar cheese, grated (reserve 3 tablespoons)
1 teaspoon salt
½ teaspoon black pepper

Peel and chop eggplant; cook in salted water until soft. Drain eggplant and mash with a fork. Sauté onion, bell pepper, and celery until tender but not brown. Mix all ingredients and place in a greased baking dish. Top with reserved cheese and breadcrumbs. Bake at 375°F for 25 minutes. Serves 6-8.

Eggplant, Quick and Easy

1 medium eggplant, young and tender
¼ cup water
2 cubes chicken bouillon
1 tomato, coarsely chopped (optional)
3 tablespoons olive oil
½ cup seasoned Italian bread crumbs
1 onion, chopped
1 rib celery, chopped
½ bell pepper, chopped
1 clove garlic, crushed
½ cup grated Mozzarella cheese

Remove stem and cut off hard area around stem of eggplant. Coarsely grate entire eggplant, including skin. Heat water in large saucepan; add bouillon. Stir until dissolved. Bring to boil and add grated eggplant and tomato, stirring in quickly. Cover, reduce heat to medium, and cook for 5 minutes. Remove from heat; toss with oil. Add crumbs. Mix. In small skillet sauté onion, celery, bell pepper, and garlic and add to eggplant mixture. Adjust seasoning. Turn into baking dish and top with cheese. Bake at 350°F till bubbly.
NOTE: This recipe is versatile. You might want to add a few shrimp or omit celery and pepper.

Baked Tomatoes au Gratin

6 firm tomatoes	3 tablespoons butter
3 tablespoons brown sugar	¼ cup bread crumbs
1½ teaspoons salt	3 slices bacon

Cut out a small well from the top of the tomatoes. Combine sugar, salt, and butter and fill each well. Lightly brown bread crumbs in remaining butter and place over top of tomato. In a small skillet fry bacon until crisp. Crumble and sprinkle over each tomato. Place the tomatoes in a well-buttered shallow baking dish. Bake them for 15 minutes in a pre-heated 400°F oven. Serves 6.

Mushroom Stuffing

1 medium onion, finely chopped	¾ teaspoon salt
2 cloves garlic, crushed	2 tablespoons Parmesan cheese
1 pound fresh mushrooms, sliced	1 tablespoon chopped parsley
½ cup margarine	Pinch of thyme
2 cups Italian breadcrumbs	Water to moisten.
½ cup olive oil	

Sauté onion and garlic in the margarine until limp. Add mushrooms and sauté 3 additional minutes. Add remaining ingredients and mix gently. Place mixture in buttered 1½ quart baking dish. Bake at 375°F until hot. Use as a vegetable side dish.

To use as stuffing, omit baking step. Stuff baking hen or small turkey with stuffing and roast fowl as usual.

Okra Medley

1 pound fresh okra, sliced into ½ to ¾ inch pieces
1 medium onion, chopped
2 plum tomatoes, diced
1 8-ounce can tomato sauce
1 teaspoon sugar
¼ teaspoon oregano or basil
¼ teaspoon Tabasco, or to taste
1 tablespoon bacon drippings or butter
Salt and pepper to taste

Combine all ingredients in a saucepan. Simmer with lid on pan until vegetables are tender, about 30 minutes.

Vegetables

Low-Fat Stuffed Baked Potatoes

2 large baking potatoes

4 slices bacon, quartered

¼ cup chopped green onions

½ cup non-fat yogurt

2 tablespoons grated Parmesan cheese

½ teaspoon salt

½ teaspoon black pepper

Bake potatoes at 400°F for 1 hour or until done. In a medium skillet, fry bacon pieces until crisp. Remove bacon and crumble. In 3 tablespoons of bacon grease, sauté onions until tender. Cut baked potatoes in half lengthwise and scoop out pulp, taking care to retain shells intact. Add pulp, bacon, yogurt, cheese, salt and pepper to sautéed onions in skillet, mixing and mashing to blend thoroughly. Stuff potato skins. Bake 15 to 20 minutes at 350°F. Serves 4.

Skillet Squash

2 pounds young, small, yellow squash, sliced

½ cup water

¾ teaspoon salt

2 slices bacon, cooked

3 tablespoons bacon grease

2 ribs celery, finely chopped

1 large onion, finely chopped

2 tablespoons finely chopped bell pepper

⅛ teaspoon garlic powder

⅛ teaspoon dried dill

In a saucepan, boil squash in lightly salted water for 10 to 15 minutes. Drain and set aside. In a large skillet, fry bacon until crisp. In 3 tablespoons of bacon grease, sauté the remaining ingredients, including the crumbled bacon. Add squash and mix well. Season the mixture with salt and pepper to taste.

NOTE: May be kept in refrigerator for several days until needed. Makes a nice casserole when sprinkled with Italian breadcrumbs and Parmesan cheese, then baked for 30 minutes at 350°F.

NOTE: 3 tablespoons olive oil may be substituted for the bacon and bacon drippings.

Sunday Dinner Spinach

2 10-ounce packages frozen, chopped spinach
4 tablespoons butter
1 onion, chopped
½ pound ham, diced
¼ teaspoon Tabasco sauce
1 3-ounce package cream cheese
½ cup grated Parmesan cheese

Cook spinach following package directions. While spinach is cooking, melt butter in medium saucepan; add chopped onion and diced ham. Cook until onions are transparent. Add spinach, Tabasco sauce, cream cheese and Parmesan cheese. Simmer, stirring often, over low heat until cheeses are well blended.

Sweet Potato Casserole

4 cups cooked, mashed sweet potatoes
(or 30-ounce can sweet potatoes, drained)
6 tablespoons butter
1 cup sugar
2 eggs
1 teaspoon vanilla
1 12-ounce can evaporated milk

Mash potatoes with butter in a mixer. In a separate bowl beat eggs, mix in sugar and vanilla. Add to mashed potatoes. Add milk and mix well. Mixture will be soupy. Pour into buttered 8×12 inch dish and bake 20 to 25 minutes in a preheated 350° to 375°F oven.

TOPPING:
¼ cup butter
¾ cup brown sugar
¾ cup lightly crushed cornflakes
1 cup chopped pecans
½ cup coconut

Cream butter and sugar together by hand. Add cornflakes, pecans, and coconut. Sprinkle on top of potato mixture. When ready to serve, heat 20 to 25 minutes in a preheated 350° to 375°F oven.

Sweet Potato Casserole With Praline Topping

3 cups sweet potatoes (about 4 good-sized ones)
½ cup sugar
½ cup butter
2 eggs, beaten
1 teaspoon vanilla
⅓ cup milk
⅛ teaspoon salt
TOPPING:
3 tablespoons (scant) soft butter
½ cup light brown sugar
¼ cup flour
Dash of salt
½ cup chopped pecans

Boil and mash potatoes. Add sugar, butter, eggs, milk and seasonings and mix well. Put in 9×13 inch greased baking dish. Mix topping ingredients together with pastry cutter and sprinkle over potato mixture. Bake 25 minutes at 350°F. Serves 12. NOTE: If canned sweet potatoes are substituted, reduce sugar to ¼ cup.

Tomatoes Rockefeller

12 thick tomato slices
2 10-ounce packages frozen chopped spinach, cooked and drained
1 cup soft breadcrumbs
1 cup seasoned breadcrumbs
1 cup finely chopped green onions
6 eggs, slightly beaten
½ cup butter, melted
½ cup grated Parmesan cheese
1 teaspoon thyme
¾ teaspoon salt
½ teaspoon minced garlic

Place tomato slices in a lightly greased 9×13 inch baking dish. Set aside. Press excess water from spinach and combine with remaining ingredients. Mound mixture on tomato slices. Bake at 350°F for 15 minutes. Cover if you don't serve it immediately. Serves 12.

Mirlitons

Many visitors to New Orleans have no idea what a mirliton (pronounced MER-leh-ton) is. It's a green, mild-flavored squash, which grows prolifically on climbing vines in the humid climate. In Florida and California, a mirliton is called a chayote (pronounced shy-O-teh). In the Caribbean, its called a chouchou. Others call it Aztec squash, mango squash, or vegetable pear.

New Orleans Style Shrimp-Stuffed Mirlitons

3 large or 4 medium mirlitons
1½ cups bread crumbs made from soft bread
4 tablespoons butter
2 cloves garlic, crushed
1 extra large or 2 medium onions, finely chopped
1 pound medium sized shrimp, coarsely chopped (each in three pieces)
1 teaspoon salt
½ teaspoon pepper
Several dashes of Tabasco sauce
1 large egg, well beaten
2 tablespoons chopped, fresh parsley
½ teaspoon ground thyme
¾ cup Italian seasoned bread crumbs

Prepare mirlitons by simmering in salted water until tender when pierced with a fork. Cool. Cut each in half and remove seeds and any stringy parts around seeds. Scoop out pulp carefully to preserve the skins intact. Reserve the skins. Coarsely chop the pulp. Drain excess water and add soft bread crumbs. Melt butter in large skillet, sauté garlic and onion over medium heat until tender, approximately 5 minutes. Add the chopped shrimp, cook ten minutes or until all shrimp are a pink color. Add mirliton pulp mixture, salt, pepper and Tabasco sauce. Taste and correct seasoning if necessary. Cook for 5 more minutes, stirring constantly. Allow mixture to cool; then add beaten egg, parsley and thyme. Mix until all ingredients are thoroughly blended. Fill the mirliton skins with mixture. Sprinkle top of each with Italian bread crumbs. Dot with butter. Bake in 375°F oven for 25-30 minutes. Yield: 6 to 8 servings.
NOTE: Eggplants may be substituted for mirlitons.

Vegetables

Stuffed Mirlitons

3 mirlitons

½ cup butter

½ pound ground ham

1 small onion, minced

1 clove garlic, crushed

1 pound shrimp, boiled and chopped

¼ teaspoon chopped parsley

¼ teaspoon dried thyme leaves

Salt

Pepper

1 cup bread crumbs

Boil mirlitons in salted water until tender, but do not overcook (about 30-40 minutes). Remove from water and cool. Melt one half of the butter in skillet. Add ham, onions and garlic and cook until onions become transparent. Slice mirlitons in half lengthwise, remove and discard seeds. Carefully scoop out pulp, leaving the shell in good condition for stuffing. Mash pulp and add to ham mixture along with shrimp, parsley and thyme. Salt and pepper to taste. Cook 10 minutes. Add ¾ cup bread crumbs, mixing well. Spoon into shells. Sprinkle the top with remaining crumbs. Dot with butter. Bake 15 minutes in a preheated 350°F oven. Serves 6.

Mirliton Casserole

9 or 10 medium mirlitons

1 pound small shrimp, peeled

1 pound crabmeat

1 bell pepper, chopped

3 medium onions, chopped

1 bunch green onions, chopped

½ cup chopped parsley

2 cloves garlic, crushed

½ cup chopped celery

Paprika

Salt and pepper

Bread crumbs

Prepare mirlitons by simmering in salted water until tender when pierced with a fork. Cool. Cut each in half and remove seed and any stringy parts and peel. Mash mirliton pulp with potato masher. Sauté mirliton pulp, chopped peppers, onions, celery, garlic, and shrimp for 20 minutes. Then add to crabmeat which has been mixed with parsley, bread crumbs and paprika. Salt and pepper to taste. Bake in 350°F oven until bubbly. Serve immediately.

THE RIVERWALK

The Riverwalk began as part of the 1984 World's Fair. Its stores and restaurants stretch for nearly half a mile along the Mississippi.

MEATS & POULTRY

Beef and Pork:

Poultry:

Red Beans

There may be fifty thousand recipes for red beans and rice, the traditional Monday dish in New Orleans. Every cook adds something different — but, on Monday, everyone eats red beans. Monday was the traditional wash-day. Until recently, washing involved boiling the clothes in a large pot on a stove or over an outside fire, on which the red beans could cook, too, carefully-watched and frequently stirred. Served with rice, they are a delicious complete protein.

Tips for Cooking Dried Beans

- Always wash and pick over the beans, to remove any stems, leaves, or small rocks.
- Cover the beans with water, and boil them for two minutes. Remove them from the heat, and let them stand at least an hour. This method retains vitamins, shortens the cooking time, and makes the beans more tender.
- Salt toughens beans. Add it toward the end of the cooking.
- A little butter or grease, if you are not using seasoning meat, will keep the beans from boiling over.
- One cup of dry beans produces about 2 to 2½ cups of cooked beans.
- If you are serving the beans with sausage, it is better to cook the sausage separately, and then put it in the beans near the end of the cooking.

Red Beans and Rice

3 quarts water
¼ teaspoon Tabasco sauce
1 teaspoon Worcestershire sauce
1 pound red beans
1 cup chopped celery
1 cup chopped onion
¼ cup chopped fresh parsley
3 cloves garlic, minced
2 bay leaves
½ pound ham, cubed
¼ pound hot sausage, sliced
½ pound smoked sausage, sliced
3 tablespoons vegetable oil
Salt and pepper to taste
Cooked rice

Wash and pick any pebbles, etc., out of red beans. Place all ingredients except salt in a large pot and bring to a low boil. Cook uncovered for two hours or more until beans are soft. Add water if needed. To get a thick, creamy sauce, mash some of the beans against the side of the pot. Add salt to taste and cook 15 more minutes. Serve over rice in large bowls, since the stew is quite liquid.

Meats & Poultry

Po' Boys

Tradition has it that the sandwich was invented by and named for a man who would rather gamble than eat, John Montagu, the Earl of Sandwich, in the early eighteenth century. It's a convenient, no-dish meal.

If most of America now eats processed meat and cheese between slices of soft, white bread, older tastes survive in "heroes", "subs", "grinders" — and the New Orleans po' boy sandwich. It's made with French bread, top-quality meats and cheeses, or seafood. It is almost always "dressed" with lettuce, tomato, and lots of mayonnaise. The most famous po' boy is the *mediatrice*, the "peacemaker", an oyster loaf presented by erring husbands to angry wives. It seems to have been made with creamed oysters in the nineteenth century, but now it features fried oysters.

A unique New Orleans sandwich is the *muffaletta* — Italian meats and cheeses, and a garlicky olive salad, in a round Sicilian loaf. Natives buy one for the family for supper. Tourists buy one per person and are overwhelmed!

Roast Beef Po' Boy "Dressed"

2-4 pound rump roast
Pepper to taste
2 tablespoons oil
6-8 garlic cloves, sliced in half
Salt to taste
1 envelope onion soup mix
2 tablespoons cornstarch
French bread
Mayonnaise
Lettuce
Sliced tomatoes

Sprinkle roast with pepper. With a small, sharp knife make slits in roast about two inches apart; place half garlic clove in each slit. Heat oil in large, heavy pot over medium heat. Brown roast well on all sides. Cover roast with hot water, add salt and pepper, cover pot and lower heat to medium low. Cook until roast is fork tender (time will depend on size of roast). Remove roast from gravy, cool, cover with foil and refrigerate. Cool and refrigerate gravy. Remove fat from top of gravy. Slice cold roast into thin slices. Add soup mix and roast slices to gravy and simmer until beef can be cut easily with a fork. Mix cornstarch with ¾ cup cold water and stir into beef and gravy. Simmer several minutes more until thickened.

To make po' boy sandwiches, cut desired length of French bread, slice in half and heat slightly in oven. Pile beef slices on one half and "dress" the other half with mayonnaise, lettuce and tomatoes. Put two halves together to make sandwich.

Beef and gravy freeze well in portion-size containers for quick po' boys in the future.

Grillades

2 to 2½ pounds round steak (beef or veal), ¼ inch thick
4 tablespoons bacon grease
salt and pepper
additional bacon grease*
¼ cup flour
1 medium onion, chopped fine
½ large bell pepper, chopped fine
½ pound fresh mushrooms, thinly sliced**
1 8-ounce can tomato sauce
1 teaspoon dried thyme
2 bay leaves
2 cloves garlic, crushed
½ cup chopped fresh parsley***
2 cups or more good claret

Trim steak of all visible fat, cut into serving pieces approximately 3 inches by 3 inches. If steak is more than ¼ inch thick, pound till ¼ inch thin. Salt and pepper meat liberally. Fry in hot bacon grease over medium heat until brown on both sides; remove meat and drain well on paper towels.

Pour remaining grease into a ¼ cup measure and add enough bacon grease to bring it to ¼ cup; return to skillet. Turn fire to medium, add flour and stir constantly until a medium brown roux forms (approximately 5 to 8 minutes). Lower heat, add chopped onion and cook for 4 minutes, stirring constantly. Add bell pepper, cook for 4 more minutes, still stirring. Add mushrooms and cook for 2 minutes, stirring constantly. The entire mixture may look strange to you the first time you cook it, but never fear — it will look and taste wonderful as the recipe progresses! Add tomato sauce, thyme, bay leaves, garlic and parsley; cook for 2 or 3 more minutes. Add a little water if sticking; just enough to help you loosen all the steak bits from the skillet. Push to side of skillet. Add 2 cups claret and stir slowly until well mixed. Add meat and any juice that has collected back to skillet. Cover and cook over a very low fire for about 1 hour, till thickened and meat is tender. Check once or twice during cooking; add more wine if liquid is needed. Serve over cooked rice or grits. Cook a day ahead of time if possible. This dish improves overnight in the refrigerator, as many Creole dishes do.

NOTE: This is one dish where you want a heavy aluminum or cast iron skillet. You WANT the bits of steak to stick — this, and the roux, form the base of a wonderful gravy.

*Vegetable oil may be substituted for bacon grease, but taste will not be as good.
**Dried mushrooms may be substituted; soak 1 cup dried mushrooms for ½ hour; rinse and drain and continue as for fresh mushrooms.
***2 tablespoons dried parsley may be substituted.

Eggplant Parmesan with Beef

1 eggplant
4 tablespoons butter or margarine
½ pound ground beef
1 tablespoon instant minced onion
1 teaspoon salt
Black pepper to taste
1 teaspoon sugar
¼ teaspoon basil leaves
¼ teaspoon oregano
1 8-ounce can tomato sauce
¼ cup grated Parmesan cheese
¼ pound Mozzarella cheese (sliced)

Peel eggplant (if desired) and cut into ½ inch slices. Melt butter in a large skillet, add eggplant in a single layer and brown lightly on both sides, adding extra butter if needed. Place in shallow 2-quart baking dish. To drippings in skillet, add ground beef, onion, salt and pepper, sugar, basil, and oregano. Mix well and cook until meat is lightly browned. Drain grease. Spoon meat mixture over eggplant. Top with tomato sauce and Parmesan cheese. Bake uncovered for 20 minutes at 350°F. Place Mozzarella slices over top of casserole and bake 10 minutes longer or until cheese is melted. NOTE: Olive oil may be substituted for butter or margarine if desired.

Lasagna

1 pound ground beef
3 eggs
1 teaspoon oregano
½ teaspoon basil
½ teaspoon garlic powder
½ teaspoon salt
16 ounces Ricotta cheese
32-ounce jar spaghetti sauce
8 ounces Mozzarella cheese, shredded
8 ounces Cheddar cheese, shredded
1-pound box lasagna noodles, uncooked
1 cup water

Brown and separate ground beef in skillet. Drain fat and juice and discard. Place eggs, oregano, basil, garlic powder, and salt in medium bowl and beat. Add ricotta cheese and mix. Combine spaghetti sauce with ground beef and mix. Spray 9×13 inch pan with cooking spray. Spread one-third of spaghetti sauce mixture in pan. Sprinkle with one-third of the shredded cheeses mixed together. Layer one-third of the uncooked noodles. Repeat the layers, ending with shredded cheese. Add water around edges. Spray a piece of foil with cooking spray and cover lasagna. Bake at 350°F for 1 hour and 15 minutes. Remove foil and bake an additional 5 minutes. Allow to cool slightly before cutting into squares.

NOTE: Cottage cheese may be substituted for ricotta cheese.

Italian Pasta with Shrimp and Sausage

2 tablespoons olive oil
2 or 3 links of Italian sausage
2 garlic cloves, minced
2 tablespoons butter
¼ cup shredded carrot
¼ cup finely chopped celery
¼ cup finely chopped onion
2 tablespoons sweet vermouth
1 pound raw shrimp, peeled and deveined
1 teaspoon salt
¼ teaspoon pepper
1 cup cream
½ teaspoon basil
½ teaspoon tarragon
½ pound thin spaghetti
½ cup grated Parmesan cheese
2 tablespoons minced parsley

Heat 1 tablespoon oil in a non-stick frying pan. Remove the sausage from the casing and fry until lightly browned. Add garlic and cook lightly. Remove meat and garlic from pan. Add the butter and vegetables to the juices in the pan, sauté lightly. Stir in the vermouth and cook 1 to 2 minutes. Remove the vegetables from the pan. Add the remaining tablespoon of oil to the pan. Add shrimp and cook until shrimp turns pink. Return the meat and vegetables to the pan. Add seasonings and cream. Heat thoroughly but do not boil. Cook spaghetti in boiling water. Drain and place in casserole. Top with shrimp and sausage mixture, Parmesan cheese and parsley.

Add 1 tablespoon of cooking oil to boiling water to prevent pasta from sticking.

Broccoli or Spinach Ground Meat Casserole

2 10-ounce packages frozen broccoli, cooked and drained
1 4-ounce can mushroom pieces
1 pound ground meat (browned and drained of fat)
1 10¾-ounce can cream of celery soup
1 8-ounce carton sour cream
¼ cup minced onion
Garlic salt and pepper to taste
8 ounces Mozzarella cheese, grated

Combine everything but cheese. Place in casserole and top with cheese. Heat in preheated 350°F oven until cheese melts and casserole is bubbly (30-45 minutes). NOTE: 2 10-ounce packages of frozen spinach may be substituted.

Brown Jambalaya

¼ cup oil
½ pound hot sausage, sliced
½ pound smoked sausage, sliced
4 large pieces of chicken, boned and cut in bite-size pieces
2 cups chopped onion
1 cup chopped celery
1 cup chopped bell pepper
2 cloves garlic, finely chopped
3 cups chicken stock*
2 teaspoons salt
cayenne pepper
2 cups long grain rice, raw
1 pound boiled shrimp, peeled (optional)
½ cup chopped green onions
¼ cup chopped parsley

In a large skillet, sauté the sausage in the oil. Remove and put into a large heavy pot (4-quart or larger). Brown the chicken in the drippings, remove, and add to large pot. Sauté the onion, celery, bell pepper, and garlic until the vegetables are tender. Add to the large pot. Add liquid to pot and bring to a boil. Add salt and pepper and the rice. Return to a boil. Cover, reduce heat to a simmer. Cook for 30-35 minutes without peeking. Add green onion, parsley and shrimp (optional). Cook and stir for five more minutes. Serves 6-8.
NOTE: Liquid to rice ratio: 1 cup raw rice to 1¼ cups liquid. Rice triples in bulk when cooked.
*Chicken stock may be made with bouillon cubes (1 cube per cup).

Italian Meatballs

3 eggs slightly beaten
½ cup milk
¼ teaspoon oregano
¼ teaspoon basil
1½ teaspoons salt
1 teaspoon pepper
2 garlic cloves, minced
1 large onion, chopped
2 ounces fresh grated Parmesan cheese
3 ribs celery, chopped
1½ cups seasoned bread crumbs
3 pounds ground meat
1 pound Italian sausage removed from casing

In a large bowl place the first eleven ingredients; mix well. Add meat and sausage. Mix well. Shape into meat balls, either cocktail size or larger. Place in 9×13 inch pan and bake at 400°F until brown, about 10 minutes.

Italian Sauce for Meatballs

¼ cup butter
1½ cups chopped onions
½ cup chopped celery
½ cup chopped green onions
½ cup chopped bell pepper
2 cloves garlic, crushed
1 32-ounce jar of prepared tomato spaghetti sauce

Melt butter. Add chopped vegetables and fry until soft. Add sauce. Simmer 1 hour. Add meatballs and simmer for another hour.

To bone chicken breasts, turn skin side down. Push against ribs of the breast until joints holding breastbone break. Push away flesh until it is just attached at the top. Pull out the breastbone and cartilage. Using a sharp-pointed knife, carefully cut meat away from rib bones. Continue cutting until wishbone is reached. Remove wishbone and remainder of rib section.

Chinese Pot Roast

2 tablespoons peanut oil
3 to 5 pound beef roast (rump or round)
1 large clove garlic, crushed
2 quarter-sized slices peeled fresh ginger
3 tablespoons dark soy sauce
3 tablespoons dry vermouth
1 cup boiling water
1 tablespoon sugar
½ teaspoon salt
Dash each of ground cloves, cinnamon, and ginger

Heat a heavy pot, just large enough to fit the roast, over high heat until hot; add oil, swirl, and heat for 30 seconds. Turn heat to medium; toss in the garlic and fresh ginger; then add the meat and brown on all sides. Add the soy sauce and wine, turning the meat a few times to coat it; then add boiling water, sugar, salt, and spices. When the liquid boils again, lower heat to maintain a slow but steady simmering; cover and simmer for 2 to 3 hours (or until fork tender, turning now and then).

To serve warm: remove the roast to a chopping board to cool and firm, then slice across the grain into desired thickness. Skim fat off the sauce and serve on the side or over the roast.

To serve cold: let the roast cool in the sauce, then refrigerate it covered. Scrape off the congealed fat. Remove the meat, cut it lengthwise into two pieces, then slice these crosswise very thinly. Spread some of the jellied sauce over the cold slices of meat.

This is also excellent for sandwiches or appetizers.

When using wine in cooking, remember the better the wine the better the dish.

Chicken Chasseur

6 chicken breasts, boned and skinned
½ cup flour, seasoned with salt and pepper
½ cup butter
½ cup oil
8 ounces mushrooms, sliced
1½ cups chopped green onions
3 tomatoes, peeled and diced
4 cloves garlic, minced
1 pinch tarragon
8 ounces white wine
1 cup chicken stock
1 teaspoon cornstarch dissolved in 1 tablespoon water
Parsley for garnish

Coat chicken with flour mixture; put in hot skillet with oil and butter and lightly brown both sides. Remove chicken. Lower heat and cook sliced mushrooms for five minutes, stirring often. Add green onions and cook for 3 to 5 minutes until tender, stirring often. Add tomatoes, garlic, and tarragon and cook 15 minutes, stirring occasionally. Add white wine and chicken stock. Cook for five more minutes. Add cornstarch dissolved in water to sauce. Stir well. Return chicken to pan and cook in sauce for 15 minutes. Add parsley before serving. Serves 6.

Marinated Chicken Breast

3 cups chicken stock
2 whole boneless chicken breasts
⅓ cup fresh lime juice
1 cup chicken stock
2 large garlic cloves, chopped
2 tablespoons fresh basil
3 green onions, chopped
⅓ cup olive oil
⅓ cup vegetable oil
¾ teaspoon sugar
½ teaspoon salt
½ to 1 teaspoon black pepper

Simmer chicken breasts in chicken stock for 8-10 minutes in a medium saucepan. Cool. Combine remaining ingredients for marinade. Slice meat. Add meat and remaining stock to marinade. Chill for 24 hours. Serves 4.

Lemon Chicken Amandine

⅓ cup lemon juice
3 tablespoons Dijon mustard
2 cloves garlic, crushed
¼ teaspoon lemon pepper
⅓ cup olive oil
6 skinless, boneless chicken breast halves, pounded to ¼-inch thickness
1 package (2½ ounces) sliced almonds
2 tablespoons butter
½ cup chicken broth
½ cup white wine
1 teaspoon cornstarch dissolved in 1 tablespoon water
2 tablespoons chopped fresh parsley
¼ teaspoon cayenne pepper
Lemon slices for garnish

Combine lemon juice, mustard, garlic and lemon pepper with olive oil. Marinate chicken breasts in this sauce in a large shallow dish for one hour at room temperature. Toast almonds on a baking sheet in a 350°F oven for 10 minutes until slightly browned. Drain chicken, reserving marinade. In a large skillet, melt butter. Add chicken and cook until slightly browned, approximately four minutes a side. Remove to a dish. Add reserved marinade, chicken broth and wine to skillet. Cook over high heat, stirring until the sauce reduces by half, about 5 minutes. Stir in cornstarch mixture, stirring until thickened and smooth. Add parsley and cayenne. Reduce heat. Return chicken to skillet and heat through. Transfer chicken to a serving plate and pour sauce over. Sprinkle toasted almonds over chicken and garnish with lemon slices. Serves 6.

Wash fresh poultry with cold running water and pat it dry before storing or cooking. Loosely wrap it in wax paper or foil. May be kept refrigerated for 1 or 2 days.

Plantation Chicken

2 tablespoons vegetable oil
1 tablespoon butter or margarine
1 medium onion, sliced
1 teaspoon tarragon leaves
1 teaspoon sweet basil leaves
½ teaspoon thyme leaves
4 whole chicken breasts, boned, skinned and split
½ pound fresh mushrooms, sliced
½ cup dry white wine
½ teaspoon salt
Dash pepper
SAUCE:
1 tablespoon butter or margarine
1 tablespoon flour
½ cup condensed chicken broth
¾ cup dry white wine
½ cup dairy sour cream
½ cup grated Parmesan cheese
1 tablespoon Creole mustard
½ teaspoon salt
Dash of pepper
1 14-ounce can artichoke hearts, sliced in half
Chopped parsley
Paprika

Heat oil and butter or margarine in large skillet; add onion, tarragon, sweet basil, and thyme. Cook until onion is tender. Add 4 chicken breasts and sauté 15 minutes, turning once. Sauté remaining 4 breasts in the same manner. After all chicken has been sautéed, add mushrooms to skillet and sauté until tender. Return all chicken to skillet, add wine, salt, and pepper; mix well. Cook over low heat, covered, for 10-15 minutes or until chicken is fork tender.

While chicken is simmering, prepare sauce. Melt butter over low heat in a 1-quart saucepan. Stir in flour until blended; gradually stir in broth and wine. Heat just to boil (about 5 minutes) stirring constantly. Reduce heat to low, and whisk in sour cream. Add cheese, mustard, salt, and pepper, stirring constantly, being careful not to boil. Remove from heat when cheese is melted; set aside. In small saucepan over low heat, heat artichokes gently in water from can; drain.

Transfer contents of skillet to a shallow baking pan, arranging chicken pieces in a single layer. Arrange artichoke hearts around chicken. Spoon wine sauce over all and run under broiler to heat thoroughly and brown (about 5-7 minutes). Top with parsley and sprinkle lightly with paprika. Makes 8 servings.
NOTE: Regular prepared mustard may be substituted if Creole mustard is not available.

Aunt Git's Turkey*

1 turkey, slightly frozen
1 or 2 sticks margarine (depending on size of turkey) sliced into tablespoons
Salt and cayenne pepper
1 onion, coarsely chopped
1 bell pepper, coarsely chopped
3 to 5 cloves garlic (amount depends on size of turkey)
6 to 10 sport peppers
2 tablespoons vinegar from the peppers
2 tablespoons salt
1 tablespoon cayenne pepper

You can use any size turkey. Aunt Git says it's easier to prepare the turkey while it is still slightly frozen. Remove the neck and giblets and rinse the turkey inside and out. Pat dry. Place on a large tray or cutting board.

Place pats of margarine in a small bowl and season generously with salt and cayenne pepper; place in freezer for several hours. Place onions, bell peppers, garlic and hot peppers into a small bowl and sprinkle lightly with more salt and cayenne pepper. Allow this to marinate for a couple of hours. In another small bowl combine 2 tablespoons salt and 1 tablespoon cayenne pepper, more if using a large turkey.

You will need a sharp pointed knife. A boning knife is perfect, preferably a 6-inch narrow one. A spoon with a thin rounded handle is also useful. Be prepared to use your hands and fingers; you may need to wear surgical gloves if your hands get irritated by pepper. The object is to season the turkey without breaking the outside skin.

Going into the cavity, take your knife, and on either side of the center breast bone, make a horizontal slit lengthwise through the center of each side of the breast, similar to one made in a pork chop that is to be stuffed. Spoon in some of the salt and pepper mixture, then with your fingers, stuff in slices of onion, bell pepper, garlic and tiny hot peppers and a little of the vinegar. Insert two to three frozen butter slices in the slit. If you have a large turkey, you will be able to make two slits on each side of the main breast bone.

With the turkey laying breast-side-up with the legs facing you, gently pull the drumstick toward you to expose the inner thigh. Gently pull the skin away from the body. Again using the boning knife, make a slit following the bone line from the top of the leg. Be careful not to cut the skin. Use your finger to make a path and repeat the stuffing procedure of above. Where the skin has been loosened on the inner thigh, spoon in the salt and cayenne mixture. Repeat on other leg.

Turn the turkey, breast-side-up with neck opening facing you. Lift the skin flap and with your knife, make a slit down the wing from the shoulder, again following the bone line.

Repeat the stuffing process on both wings. Season the outside of the turkey with salt and cayenne pepper. Any seasonings, onions, bell pepper, garlic and hot peppers that are left can be placed into the cavity along with any frozen butter pieces. Secure the wings by folding the lower part over the drumette part. Then tie the legs together with twine.

Place turkey in large roasting pan (the kind with a lid). Do not put any oil into the pan. Preheat the oven 400°F. Place the turkey into the oven uncovered and cook for 15 to 20 minutes to start the browning process. Then lower oven temperature to 350°F and cover with lid. Bake time is: for 8-9 pound turkey, 2 to 2½ hours; 12 pounds, 3 to 3½ hours; 18 to 20 pound turkey, 4 to 4½ hours. Baste with pan drippings. Do not overcook or the meat will be dry.

NOTE: Sport peppers are the small green hot peppers packed in vinegar.

SUGGESTION: After carving, return turkey to pan drippings and allow to soak for a few minutes. Any leftover meat can be used to make a great gumbo. Add drippings to gumbo pot.

*Credit: Marcelle Bienvenu, *Creole Cooking* columnist for the
New Orleans Times Picayune newspaper.

Meats & Poultry

THIS IS THE TRADITIONAL FOOD TO TAKE TO PARADES, PICNICS, BALL GAMES, AND SUMMER OUTINGS...ENJOY!

Spicy New Orleans Fried Chicken

1 frying chicken, cut up (2½ to 3 pounds)
1 teaspoon spicy seasoned salt
1 teaspoon fried chicken seasoning
1 teaspoon cayenne pepper
1 tablespoon paprika
1 teaspoon lemon pepper seasoning
1 teaspoon garlic puree
1 teaspoon Worcestershire sauce
1 tablespoon olive oil
½ cup buttermilk
1 pinch baking powder
1 cup flour
vegetable oil for frying

Cut up chicken and wash each piece well; wipe dry. Mix together all seasonings, garlic puree, olive oil and buttermilk, using a whisk or fork to mix seasonings into liquid. Using a large bowl, place chicken pieces in the liquid seasoning and mix well with your hands, rubbing liquid into chicken. Allow to stand, refrigerated and covered, for at least 2 hours, preferably overnight. Turn chicken 2 or 3 times during standing period with your hands, working liquid into chicken each time.

Place flour on large piece of waxed paper, stir in the baking powder with a fork, distributing well. Remove chicken from refrigerator; do not drain or wipe dry. Almost all of the liquid seasoning mix should be absorbed or clinging to the chicken pieces. Roll each piece of chicken in flour, coating well; shake off excess.

Use an iron or heavy aluminum skillet for frying. Heat oil on low to very hot, but not boiling (test with a cube of bread; if it browns immediately, oil is hot enough). Place chicken pieces in oil a few at a time so as not to lower temperature, starting with dark meat pieces first. Do not crowd pieces. Part of the chicken (at least ⅓) should protrude above the oil. Cook on low 10 to 15 minutes on each side until golden brown and well done. Check often. Do not turn for the first 5 minutes on each side. Drain on paper towels.

NOTE: Sweet milk may be substituted for buttermilk, but buttermilk is better.

IF GRAVY IS DESIRED, drain all but 2 tablespoons of oil from skillet. Add 1 green onion, chopped, 1 clove of garlic, chopped, a couple of shakes of black pepper, 1 teaspoon salt, and a shake of paprika. On a low fire, slowly stir in 2 tablespoons of flour, stirring constantly for approximately 5 minutes. Slowly add 1½ to 2 cups water and a dash of Worcestershire sauce; stir until well thickened. For a traditional southern gravy, substitute milk for water to produce "Milk Gravy." Serve gravy over rice or mashed potatoes.

Seafood

SECTION VI

IRON GRILL-WORK
AND BALCONIES

Beautiful cast iron-work is common in New Orleans. It was
pre-fabricated and sold from catalogues, and offered a
handsome, weatherproof alternative to wooden porches
and railings.

SEAFOOD

To serve boiled shrimp, crabs, or crawfish the way it's done in New Orleans, cover the table with several layers of brown paper or newspaper. Serve the boiled seafood on large trays. In the middle of the table, put catsup, horseradish, lemon wedges, and Worcestershire sauce, with small bowls or paper cups. Let each person serve his own seafood and mix his own sauce. Boil red potatoes and corn on the cob in the water the seafood was cooked in, and serve them as side-dishes. The only other things you need are crackers, plenty of your favorite beverage, and LOTS of paper towels. Messy, but fun!

Boiled Seafood

1 bag commercial crab boil
3 quarts water
4 tablespoons salt
1 lemon, quartered
Cayenne pepper to taste.

Mix all ingredients. Bring to a boil and continue boiling for 5 minutes. Add seafood.

For shrimp. Add approximately 4 pounds of shrimp. Bring to a boil, boiling 5 minutes. Cover, turn off heat and let shrimp stand in the seasoned water for 30 minutes. Remove from pot and let cool. The water may be used to cook corn and red potatoes to serve along with the shrimp.

For crab. 1 dozen crabs. Crabs must be alive when put into the boiling liquid. Boil for 20 minutes.

For Crawfish. 4 pounds of crawfish. As with the crab, crawfish must be alive when added to the pot. Cook for 10 minutes, and follow instructions for shrimp.

Boil only live crawfish. A straight crawfish tail indicates that the crawfish was not alive when boiled.

Seafood

Seafood and Fettuccine

4 tablespoons butter
3 tablespoons minced onion
¼ cup sliced mushrooms
¼ cup diced bell pepper
¼ cup diced sweet red pepper
4 tablespoons butter
2 tablespoons flour
1 cup chicken broth
1½ cups half-and-half
¼ cup Parmesan cheese
½ teaspoon dry mustard
Dash of cayenne pepper
½ teaspoon seafood seasoning (optional)
¼ pound crabmeat
½ pound scallops

In a small saucepan sauté the onion, mushrooms, and peppers in butter and set aside. Blend 4 tablespoons of butter and the flour until smooth. Add broth and cream, stirring well until smooth and creamy. Mix cheese, seasonings and seafood together and stir into the cream mixture. Simmer 5-7 minutes. If sauce gets too thick, add more broth. Add sautéed vegetables and heat thoroughly. Serve over plain or spinach fettuccine. Serves 4-6.

Blend of the Bayou Seafood Casserole

1 8-ounce package cream cheese
½ cup margarine or butter
1 pound shrimp, peeled
1 large onion, chopped
2 ribs celery, chopped
2 tablespoons butter
1 10¾-ounce can cream of mushroom soup
1 4-ounce can mushrooms, drained
1 tablespoon garlic salt
1 teaspoon Tabasco sauce
½ teaspoon red pepper
1 pint crab meat
¾ cup cooked rice
Sharp cheese, grated
Cracker crumbs

Melt cream cheese and butter using double boiler. Meanwhile sauté shrimp, onion, and celery in 2 tablespoons butter; add to cream cheese mixture. Add soup, mushrooms, seasonings, crab meat, and rice. Mix well, place in 2-quart casserole and top with cheese and cracker crumbs. Bake at 350°F about 20 to 30 minutes until bubbly. Serves 8. Freezes well.

Crab Patties (or Stuffed Crab Filling)

good

½ cup Italian seasoned bread crumbs
1 pound white crab meat (free of shell fragments)
1 tablespoon mayonnaise
1 tablespoon cream
1 tablespoon prepared mustard
1 egg, beaten
1 tablespoon minced parsley
1 teaspoon black pepper
½ teaspoon salt
½ teaspoon Worcestershire sauce
½ teaspoon Tabasco sauce
Additional seasoned bread crumbs
½ cup oil for frying

Gently blend ½ cup crumbs with crab meat. Set aside. Thoroughly combine next nine ingredients and add to crab and crumb mixture. Mix gently but thoroughly. Shape mixture into six patties. Heat oil in a large skillet. Coat each side of patties in additional crumbs. Fry 3 to 5 minutes on each side until crisp and brown.

If mixture is used as stuffing, clean shells thoroughly inside and out before filling them. Top with additional crumbs, dot with butter and bake in preheated 350°F oven for 15 to 20 minutes.

When frying seafood, the seafood and the batter must both be cold and the oil extremely hot. This prevents the batter from becoming saturated with grease. Cook only a few pieces at a time.

Seafood

Soft-Shell Crab

"The ultimate delight in seafood" is the well-deserved reputation of the soft-shell crab in New Orleans and other gourmet cities of the United States. Contrary to some beliefs, they are not a separate breed, but the same familiar blue crab at the molting stage. Crabs outgrow their shells, burst out of the old ones, and grow new ones. For the few hours after the "buster" crab has shed its old shell, the crab's shell is soft. This is the "magic stage" prized by crabbers and gourmets alike.

TO CLEAN THE SOFT-SHELL CRAB:

To clean the soft-shell crab, place it on a cutting surface. Lift the shell at the points on either side of the back and remove the feathery gills. Cut off the eyes and mouth. Lift the shell gently and remove the sandbag from under the mouth. Discard all the removed parts, wash the crab in cold running water, and pat it dry with paper towels.

If you are lucky enough to acquire a big batch of soft-shell crabs at one time, they may be frozen, but do not clean them before freezing. This speeds up deterioration. The crabs should be cleaned just before cooking. For freezing, simply rinse them with cold water, pat them dry, wrap them in freezer paper, and freeze quickly.

Fried Soft-Shell Crabs

6 Soft-Shell Crabs, cleaned
1 cup milk
1 egg
Salt and freshly ground pepper to taste
1½ cups flour
Cooking oil
Lemon wedges
Tartar Sauce

In a large bowl beat together the milk and egg until well blended. Season the crabs with the salt and pepper. Soak the crabs in the milk mixture for 15 minutes, turning frequently. Dredge the crabs in the flour and shake off the excess flour. In a deep fryer or large pot heat the oil to 365°F or very hot, but not boiling. Lower the crabs into the oil, being careful not to overcrowd the pot. The crabs should have room to float on the surface of the oil. Fry the crabs for 5 to 6 minutes, or until they are golden brown. Transfer the crabs to paper towels to drain. Serve the crabs piping hot, accompanied by lemon wedges and tartar sauce.

Crawfish Étouffée

1 large onion, finely chopped
1 large bell pepper, finely chopped
2 ribs celery, finely chopped
4 ounces butter
1 pound crawfish tails
2 cloves garlic, minced
Salt, red, and black pepper
4 ounces crawfish fat (if available)
Roux (optional) (See Roux)
Green onions and parsley, finely chopped

In a medium skillet, melt the butter. Add onions, bell pepper, and celery and sauté until transparent but not brown, being careful not to let butter burn. Add crawfish fat, cook for 10 minutes. Add crawfish tails, cook 5 more minutes. Add minced garlic; season to taste with salt, red and black pepper. Add walnut-sized lump of roux if desired for flavor or to stretch. Garnish with green onions and parsley. Serve over steamed rice. Serves 4.

Crawfish Pie

1 large onion, minced
½ cup minced green onion
2 cloves garlic, minced
½ bell pepper, minced
2 ribs celery, minced
¼ cup butter
1 10¾ ounce can cream of celery soup
4 tablespoons tomato sauce
1 pound coarsely minced crawfish tails
¼ cup minced parsley
½ cup seasoned bread crumbs
1 teaspoon salt
¼ teaspoon red pepper
¼ teaspoon black pepper
1 egg, beaten
¾ cup milk
Double crust for 10-inch pie

In a large skillet, sauté onions, garlic, bell pepper and celery in butter until limp. Add soup, tomato sauce, crawfish and parsley. Cook slowly for 10 minutes. Remove from heat. Add bread crumbs, salt, pepper and egg. Mix well, add milk and mix again. Bake in double crust for 40 to 50 minutes at 350°F. Can also be baked in single crust shell or individual pie shells.

Alligator Sauce Piquante*

½ pound lard
2 pounds alligator meat
Joe's Stuff or a good Creole seasoning
1 cup flour
2 cups chopped onions
2 cups chopped celery
2 cups chopped bell pepper
1 tablespoon chopped garlic
1 29-ounce can tomato sauce
1 29-ounce can crushed tomatoes
2-3 tablespoons dark brown sugar, to taste
2 cups chicken stock or water with bouillon cubes
2-3 bay leaves
1 teaspoon thyme
1 teaspoon oregano
2 teaspoons sweet basil
1-2 teaspoons salt
1-2 teaspoons cayenne pepper

Season the meat well with Joe's Stuff or Creole seasoning, and brown in lard. Remove the meat and make a roux using the fat and an equal amount of flour, cooking it to a medium brown color. Add onions, celery, and bell pepper. When pot is cooled somewhat, add garlic and sauté vegetables over medium heat until tender. Add tomato sauce, crushed tomatoes, chicken stock, and enough brown sugar to cut the acid taste of the tomatoes. Season to your own taste and simmer until thickened and meat is tender. Serve over rice. Enjoy! Serves 8-10.

*Recipe courtesy of Joe Cahn of the New Orleans School of Cooking,
 620 Decatur Street (inside the Jackson Brewery).

Golden Crabmeat au Gratin

1½ cups finely chopped onion
2 ribs celery, finely chopped
¾ cup butter or margarine
¾ cup flour
2½ cups evaporated milk
3 egg yolks
1 teaspoon salt
½ teaspoon cayenne pepper
¼ teaspoon black pepper
1 pound white crabmeat
¾ pound grated cheddar cheese

In a large skillet, sauté onions and celery in butter until onions are wilted. Blend in flour. Over low heat, pour in milk gradually, stirring constantly. Stir salt, red and black pepper into egg yolks and add to mixture. Cook for 5 minutes or until well blended and thickened. Remove from heat. Gently fold in crabmeat. Transfer to 8 lightly greased ramekins or one large casserole. Cover with grated cheese and bake in 375°F oven for 15-20 minutes or until light gold and bubbly. Serves 8.

Crawfish Fettuccine

1½ cups butter
3 medium onions, chopped
3 ribs celery, chopped
2 bell peppers, chopped
¼ cup flour
⅓ cup parsley flakes
2 pounds peeled crawfish tails
1 pint half-and-half
½ cup white wine
1 pound Velveeta cheese, in ½-inch cubes
2 tablespoons chopped and seeded jalapeno peppers
3 garlic cloves, crushed
Zatarain's Creole Seasoning*
1 pound fettuccine noodles
1 tablespoon olive oil
½ cup Parmesan cheese

Melt butter in heavy skillet. Add onions, celery and bell peppers. Cook 10 minutes until soft. Add flour and blend well. Cover and cook 15 minutes over low heat, stirring occasionally. Add parsley and crawfish tails. Cover and cook 20 minutes, stirring often. Add half-and-half, wine, cheese, jalapenos and garlic. Mix well. Add Creole Seasoning to taste. Cook noodles according to package instructions. Drain and add one tablespoon olive oil and Parmesan cheese. Combine both mixtures and pour into a 3-quart buttered casserole. Bake at 350°F for 12 minutes until hot and bubbly. Serves 12-16.

*Creole Seasoning Blend may be substituted (see Section VII).

Crawfish Pasta Casserole

2 onions, chopped
2 ribs celery, chopped
1 bell pepper, chopped
3 green onions, thinly sliced
3 cloves garlic, finely chopped
¾ cup butter
2 pounds peeled crawfish tails*
1 tablespoon flour
1 tablespoon chopped parsley
½ teaspoon seasoned salt
1½ cups half-and-half
¼ pound jalapeno cheese
8 ounces pasta, cooked
Parmesan cheese

In a large saucepan sauté onions, celery, pepper, green onions and garlic in butter for 15 minutes. Add the seafood, flour, parsley and salt and sauté another 15 minutes. Add the half-and-half and cheese. Heat until cheese is melted and blended. Toss with pasta. Place in lightly greased casserole and sprinkle with Parmesan cheese. Bake for 15 minutes at 350°F.

NOTE: This recipe may be served in small portions as an appetizer as well as an entree.

*Boiled shrimp may be substituted.

Oysters Bienville

1 slice bacon, diced
1 large garlic clove, minced
3 large fresh mushrooms, chopped
3 green onions, chopped
2 tablespoons butter
3 tablespoons flour
½ cup half-and-half
¼ cup oyster juice
Dash lemon juice
1 tablespoon brandy
½ cup chopped cooked shrimp
1 tablespoon chopped parsley
Salt
Tabasco sauce
1 dozen oysters on the half shell

Fry bacon until clear. Add garlic, mushrooms, green onions, and fry until bacon is browned. Add butter, blend in flour to make a roux. Cook slowly for 20 minutes, then add cream gradually. When thickened, blend in lemon juice, oyster juice and brandy. Add shrimp and parsley, gently simmer for 3 minutes. Season to taste with salt and Tabasco sauce. Arrange a dozen oyster shells on a bed of rock salt in a baking pan. Warm slightly in a 300°F oven. Place an oyster on each shell, cover with sauce, put under a broiler until bubbly hot. Yield: 1 dozen.
NOTE: May add Parmesan cheese for a slightly different taste.

Oysters and Artichokes

¼ cup butter
1 large onion, chopped
½ teaspoon thyme leaves
¾ teaspoon oregano
3 cloves garlic, crushed
2 tablespoons chopped parsley
¼ teaspoon red pepper
1 teaspoon lemon pepper
1 dozen oysters, reserve liquor
1 14-ounce can quartered artichoke hearts, drained
1 cup Italian bread crumbs
½ cup freshly grated Parmesan cheese
¼ cup olive oil

In a skillet melt butter. Add the onions and sauté until limp. Add all of the seasonings and mix well. Add the oysters, and when the edges curl, add the oyster liquor. Add the artichoke hearts to the oysters. Fold in bread crumbs. Transfer mixture to a buttered casserole or 4 ramekins. Sprinkle heavily with Parmesan cheese. Dot with olive oil. Bake for 15 to 20 minutes at 350°F. Serves 4.

Oysters en Brochette

Large oysters
Bacon slices

Begin with the same number of oysters and bacon slices. In skillet on top of stove, partially cook bacon, turning once, until half-cooked, but still pliable. Wrap each oyster in a slice of bacon, securing with a toothpick. Place on rack in pan and cook at 450°F under broiler, turning once, until bacon is done and crisp. Serve on toast points.

Seafood

Fried Oysters

½ cup flour
½ cup corn meal
½ teaspoon baking powder
1 teaspoon salt
1 egg, beaten
2 tablespoons milk
Few drops Tabasco sauce
2 dozen large oysters

Combine flour, corn meal, baking powder and salt. In separate dish, combine egg, milk, and Tabasco sauce. Dip oysters into dry mixture, into egg mixture, and back into dry mixture. Put oysters into refrigerator for at least 20 minutes or until well chilled. Fry in deep hot fat (375°F) until golden brown. Drain on absorbent paper towel.

NOTE: Seafood fries better and absorbs less oil if it is cold when put into the hot oil.

Creole Barbecued Shrimp

1½ cups butter
3-4 pounds fresh, unpeeled shrimp, preferably heads on
4 ounces warm beer
1 teaspoon chopped garlic
6 teaspoons Creole Seasoning Blend (see Section VII)
1 teaspoon rosemary
2 teaspoons black pepper
½ teaspoon Worcestershire sauce
2 teaspoons lemon juice

Melt 1 cup butter in skillet and add shrimp, beer, garlic, seasoning, rosemary, black pepper, and Worcestershire. Sauté for 2-3 minutes or until pepper begins adhering to shell and shell begins separating from meat. Add remaining butter. To avoid breaking shrimp, agitate the skillet from side to side to mix ingredients. Add lemon juice. Serve when butter completely melts. 4-6 servings. Peel, eat and enjoy. Best served with French bread for dunking, or serve drippings over rice.

NOTE: Seafood cooked in the shell needs more seasoning than when cooked after peeling.

Shrimp Marigny

1 pound raw, jumbo shrimp, peeled and deveined
½ teaspoon salt
½ teaspoon olive oil
3 garlic cloves, crushed
½ cup brandy
1 cup half and half
1 small onion, minced
8 ounces sliced fresh mushrooms
2 tablespoons butter
¼ teaspoon white pepper
½ teaspoon oregano
½ cup white wine
2 16-ounce cans tomatoes, drained and chopped
2 tablespoons corn starch
2 tablespoons cold water

Split the shrimp down the back and sprinkle with salt. In a large heavy skillet heat the oil. Add the garlic and shrimp and cook for five minutes. Add the brandy and cream and stir constantly. Sauté onions and mushrooms in butter. Add to shrimp mixture along with pepper, oregano, wine and tomatoes. Thicken with cornstarch, which has been dissolved in cold water. Serve over noodles. Serves 6.

Sautéed Shrimp

3 tablespoons butter or margarine
1 tablespoon minced parsley
2 tablespoons minced celery
1 clove garlic, minced
1½ pounds shelled, deveined raw shrimp
¼ cup white wine
½ teaspoon salt
⅛ teaspoon white pepper
2 drops Tabasco sauce, or to taste

Melt butter or margarine in a skillet; add parsley, celery, garlic, and shrimp. Cook over low heat, stirring occasionally, just until shrimp turn pink and curl — about 10 minutes. Add the wine, salt, pepper, and Tabasco; cook for 2 minutes more, stirring constantly. Serve with rice. Also good with mashed potatoes. Serves 4.

Seafood

Simple Shrimp Creole

2 tablespoons butter or margarine
½ cup minced onion
2 tablespoons flour
1 bay leaf, crushed
¼ cup diced celery
1 teaspoon minced parsley
½ cup minced bell pepper
Dash of cayenne
¼ teaspoon Tabasco sauce
½ teaspoon salt
1 6¼ ounce can tomato paste
3 cups water
2 cups cooked shrimp
1 cup rice, cooked

In a large heavy skillet, melt the butter. Add the onion and sauté until limp, but not brown. Blend in the flour. Add the bay leaf, celery, parsley, bell pepper, cayenne, Tabasco sauce, salt, tomato paste, and water. Cook for 20 minutes over low heat, stirring occasionally, until thickened. Stir in the shrimp and simmer for 20 minutes. Serve over rice. Serves 4.

Skillet Shrimp Creole

½ cup diced celery
1 medium onion, chopped
½ cup diced bell pepper
3 tablespoons butter
1 8-ounce can tomato sauce
1 8-ounce can water
1 16-ounce can tomatoes
1 teaspoon sugar
1 bay leaf
½ teaspoon garlic powder
¼ teaspoon Worcestershire sauce
Tabasco sauce to taste
1 pound peeled raw shrimp
1 cup rice, cooked

Sauté celery, onion, and bell pepper in butter until tender. Add all remaining ingredients except rice. Simmer until shrimp turns pink. Serve over cooked rice. Serves 3-4.

Chef Paul Prudhomme's Blackening Method*

The "blackening" method (using an intensely hot cast-iron skillet) was created by Chef Paul Prudhomme to try to create the taste of cooking directly over an open fire.

Blackening changes the texture of fish and meat and provides a building of natural tastes that can't be duplicated by any other cooking method. Butter and herbs and spices are the elements that allow the blackening method to reach its ultimate potential. They form a barrier between the fish or meat and the hot skillet. The extreme heat and the resulting evaporation of the surface juices of the fish or meat also keep the fish or meat suspended slightly off the skillet bottom and, in addition, make the surface of the fish or meat sweet — that is, the butter, seasonings, evaporation and heat keep the fish or meat suspended slightly off the skillet bottom and keep the surface sweet. Only the surface juices from the fish or meat evaporate and cause steam and this concentrates the outer fibers of the fish or meat into a thin crust and accents the taste of the fish or meat in the same way that the reduction of a stock or cream accents the taste. The blackened fish and blackened meat are wonderfully juicy and tender because the blackened surfaces seal in the natural juices of the fish and meat.

The following points are helpful to remember:

1. Cast iron is the best cooking material or container.

2. The skillet temperature should be close to 700 degrees.

3. Dipping the fish or meat in butter or margarine and then sprinkling on the herbs and spices are essential steps because the butter and seasonings form a layer in between the hot black skillet and the fish or meat.

4. The seasonings must be sprinkled on evenly (as you would salt). If too much seasoning is present, it destroys the method of cooking.

5. When the fish or meat is first put in the pan, there may be a flame flare up because of the intense heat. If this does not die out immediately, cover the pan for 30 seconds to smother the flame.

6. When cooking more than one batch of fish or meat, the skillet should be thoroughly wiped out in between the first three batches to remove all burned particles and oil — or these will produce a burned taste.

7. The blackening method should be done either outdoors or in a commercial kitchen (with strong vents); the process creates an incredible amount of smoke that will set off your own and your neighbors' smoke alarms.

8. A butane burner or gas grill works well; if you use charcoal, blow the coals with a hair dryer to make the heat more intense and add 12 to 14 chunks of hickory or other hard wood to the coals — and continue to add more wood as it burns up.

9. If you feel that your fire is not intense, or if you get a cool down in the skillet after the first batch, let your fish or meat come to room temperature just before cooking.

10. Bronzing is the same thing as blackening, but you just don't use as much heat and it can be done inside. The fish or meat will become bronze in color. The pan does not need to be as hot as it does when blackening food. Cast iron is not necessary; a heavy pan will work fine.

11. Fresh fish fillets or fish steaks (firm-fleshed) should be one-half to three-fourths inch thick; pork chops should be one-half to three-fourths inch thick (and don't be afraid to serve the chops pink); steaks and lamb chops should be at least three-fourths to one-inch thick or thicker (if you like yours pink); hamburger patties should be three-fourths to one-inch thick; chicken pieces should be boned and flattened with a mallet to about one-half inch thick.

*Courtesy of Chef Paul Prudhomme of K-Paul's Louisiana Kitchen

Chef Paul Prudhomme's Blackened Fish*

If you don't have a commercial hood vent over your stove, this dish will set off your and your neighbor's smoke alarms! It's better to cook it outdoors on a gas grill or a butane burner. Or, you can use a charcoal grill, but you'll need to make the coals hotter by giving them extra air. (A normal charcoal fire doesn't get hot enough to "blacken" the fish properly.) Meanwhile, heat your cast-iron skillet as hot as possible on your kitchen stove, at least 10 minutes. When the coals are glowing, use very thick potholders to carefully transfer the hot skillet to the grill.

This dish is also great cooked directly in the flames on a charcoal or gas grill. When the coals are glowing, add some chunks of hickory or other hardwood to get a flame for cooking; have the flames reaching above the grates before putting on the fish. As the wood burns up, continue to add more wood chunks.

3 tablespoons Chef Paul Prudhomme's Blackened Redfish Magic
¾ pound (3 sticks) unsalted butter, melted
6 (8- to 10-ounce) redfish fillets (or other firm-fleshed fish such as pompano, tilefish, golden tile, red snapper, wall-eyed pike or sac-a-lait) or salmon or tuna steaks (or other freshwater or saltwater fish), cut about ½ inch thick (see Note)

NOTE: Redfish and pompano are ideal for this method of cooking. If tilefish is used, you may have to split the fillets in half horizontally to have the proper thickness. If you can't get any of these fish, red snapper, wall-eyed pike or sac-a-lait fillets or salmon or tuna steaks can be substituted. In any case, the fillets or steaks must not be more than ¾ inch thick.

Heat a large cast-iron skillet over very high heat until it is beyond the smoking stage and you see white ash in the skillet bottom, at least 10 minutes. Meanwhile, pour 2 tablespoons melted butter in each of 6 small ramekins; set aside and keep warm. Reserve the remaining butter.

Heat the serving plates in a 250° oven.

Dip each fillet in the reserved melted butter so that both sides are well coated; then sprinkle the Blackened Redfish Magic generously and evenly on both sides of the fillets, patting it in by hand. Place 1 or 2 fillets in skillet and pour 1 teaspoon melted butter on top of each (be careful, as the butter may flame up). Cook uncovered over very high heat until the underside becomes deep-brown, almost black (but not burned), about 2 minutes (the time may vary according to the fillet's thickness and the heat of the skillet). Turn the fish over and pour 1 teaspoon more butter on top of each; cook till fish is done, about 2 minutes more. Repeat with remaining fillets. Serve each fillet while piping hot. To serve, place one fillet and a ramekin of butter on each plate. Makes 6 servings.

*Recipe courtesy of Chef Paul Prudhomme of K-Paul's Louisiana Kitchen

Trout Amandine

¼ cup oil
Salt and pepper
4 trout fillets approximately 8 ounces each
½ cup flour
½ cup butter
Juice of 1 lemon
¼ cup white wine
1 dash Worcestershire sauce
½ cup sliced almonds

Pour oil into skillet. Salt and pepper trout, dip both sides in flour, and place fillets in hot (375°F) oil. Cook about 5 minutes on each side. When cooked remove fillets to heated platter and discard oil. To the same skillet add butter and heat until it is lightly browned. Remove from heat and add lemon juice, wine and Worcestershire sauce. Return to fire, add almonds and cook for 1 minute or until almonds brown. Spoon over trout fillets and garnish with lemon wedges and parsley.

Seafood

Trout Supreme

4 large fish fillets (preferably trout and seasoned to taste)
1 can frozen cream of shrimp soup, thawed
Grated Parmesan cheese
¼ fresh lemon

Grease a 10×14 inch baking dish with butter. Line it with a single layer of seasoned fish fillets. Pour soup over fish. Sprinkle grated Parmesan cheese generously over top. Squeeze lemon over all. Place uncovered in 350°F oven for about 35 minutes or until it is bubbling and creamy. Serves 4.
NOTE: If frozen soup is unavailable, canned soup may be substituted.

Courtbouillon

1 or 2 large red snapper, grouper, or other firm flesh fish, cut into serving-sized pieces
3 pounds shrimp, cleaned and deveined
4 dozen oysters (strain and set aside, saving water)
1½ cups flour
¾ cup vegetable oil
½ cup margarine
3 small bunches green onions, chopped
5 cloves garlic, chopped
1 cup chopped celery
Generous pinch thyme
Generous pinch rosemary
3 bay leaves if desired
1 16-ounce can tomatoes or sauce
2 lemons, cut in half (remove seeds)
¾ cup chopped parsley

To prepare roux, brown flour in vegetable oil and margarine in heavy saucepan until golden brown, stirring constantly. Add green onions, garlic, celery, thyme, and rosemary. Cook until soft; add tomatoes, oyster water, and bay leaves (add more water if needed, but keep sauce thick). Add lemons and parsley and cook for about 1 hour. Place fish in deep, open baking pan with slice of lemon on each piece. Salt and pepper and pour a little melted margarine over fish and bake in 350°F oven. When fish begins to cook add oysters and shrimp to sauce. (Be sure to examine oysters for gritty pieces before adding.) Pour sauce over fish and bake until fish is cooked, approximately 45 minutes to 1 hour.

Baked Redfish Creole

2 onions, minced
1 bell pepper, minced
4½-ounce can mushrooms, drained and chopped
2 cloves garlic, minced
2 tablespoons olive oil
1 10-ounce can Rotel tomatoes
1 16-ounce can stewed tomatoes
1 8-ounce can tomato sauce
2 bay leaves
4 to 5 pounds of redfish
¼ teaspoon salt
⅛ teaspoon cayenne pepper
1 cup white wine
parsley and lemon wedges for garnish

Cook onions, pepper, mushrooms, and garlic in olive oil until wilted. Add tomatoes, tomato sauce, and bay leaves and simmer for about 30 minutes. Season fish well with salt and cayenne pepper. Place in well greased baking dish and add wine. Cover with sauce and cook approximately 30 minutes in a 350°F oven. Garnish with parsley and lemon wedges. Serves 6.

Baked Catfish Deluxe

4 catfish fillets (1 pound)
¼ cup lemon juice
¼ teaspoon Italian seasoning
¼ teaspoon salt
⅛ teaspoon pepper
Vegetable cooking spray
½ cup chopped green onions
1 medium sweet red pepper, chopped
1 clove garlic, minced
1 medium tomato, diced
1 cup shredded Mozzarella cheese

Rinse fillets in cold water and pat dry. Place into a shallow dish. Pour lemon juice over fillets, sprinkle with Italian seasoning, salt and pepper. Cover and refrigerate for one hour. Coat a large skillet with cooking spray. Heat skillet and add onions, red pepper and garlic; sauté until vegetables are tender. Add tomato and sauté until tomato is hot. Remove from heat and drain. Remove fillets from lemon juice and place in an 8×12×2 inch baking dish. Spread sautéed vegetables over fillets. Bake in a preheated 350°F oven for 30 minutes or until fish flakes easily when tested. Sprinkle cheese over fillets and place back into oven just until cheese melts.

Seafood

Broiled Trout Fillets

4 trout fillets (approximately 1 pound)
½ teaspoon salt
¼ teaspoon white pepper
½ cup butter, melted
2 green onions, white part only, finely chopped
1 clove garlic, finely minced
½ teaspoon finely minced ginger
1 teaspoon tarragon, crushed
¼ teaspoon cayenne pepper
juice of 1 lemon
1 teaspoon Worcestershire sauce
1 teaspoon Zatarain's Creole seasoning

Season fillets with salt and pepper. Place in a buttered baking dish. Melt butter in small skillet; add green onions and sauté for 2 minutes; add garlic and ginger and sauté for an additional minute. Remove from heat; add tarragon, cayenne pepper, lemon juice, Worcestershire sauce and Creole seasoning. Stir well and spoon over trout fillets.

Place under broiler (7 to 10 inches from heat source) and broil for 10 to 15 minutes, or until fish is done. Fish is done when it flakes easily when tested with a fork. If Zatarain's Creole seasoning is not available, you may substitute Creole seasoning mix. See section VII for recipe.

Fish Butter (Microwave)

Use to baste baked or broiled fish, or other seafood, broiled steaks, or chicken, etc. Also makes great garlic bread when spread on French bread slices before heating.

2 cups butter or margarine, melted, warm
½ cup minced green onions
2 large cloves garlic, finely minced
1 teaspoon finely minced ginger
2 teaspoons crushed, dried tarragon
½ teaspoon cayenne pepper
Juice of two lemons
1½ teaspoons Worcestershire sauce
1 tablespoon Zatarain's Creole seasoning*

In a 4-cup glass measuring cup, combine all ingredients and heat in the microwave at ½ power until it starts bubbling. Stir well and allow to cool, stirring occasionally to mix ingredients evenly.
NOTE: This will keep two weeks in the refrigerator. It also freezes well.

*Creole Seasoning Blend may be substituted (see Section VII)

Baked Stuffed Flounder

STUFFING FOR 4 FLOUNDERS:
½ cup butter (divided)
¾ cup minced onion
¼ cup chopped green onion
2 celery ribs, chopped fine
1 cup peeled and chopped raw shrimp
½ cup chopped fresh mushrooms (4 ounce can)
¾ cup fresh crabmeat
2 tablespoons minced parsley
1 tablespoon Worcestershire sauce
¼ cup half-and-half
¾ cup seasoned bread crumbs
½ teaspoon Creole Seasoning Blend (see Section VII—page 88)
2 tablespoons olive oil
2 tablespoons lemon juice
⅓ cup white wine
Paprika, lemon wedges, and parsley for garnish

In a large skillet, sauté onion and green onion in ¼ cup butter until soft. Add celery and sauté 3 minutes longer. Add shrimp and mushrooms and sauté until shrimp are pink. Add crabmeat, parsley, Worcestershire sauce, half-and-half, bread crumbs, and Creole Seasoning Blend, and stir well. Slit the skin of the flounders on the dark side, lengthwise down center. On both sides of the slit, form pockets by running the knife between the skin and the meat. Fill pockets with stuffing. Place flounders in a buttered shallow baking pan. Melt remaining butter then add oil and lemon juice. Brush fish with this mixture. Sprinkle with paprika. Bake at 350°F for 25 minutes. Spoon wine over each flounder and bake 5 minutes. Serve garnished with lemon wedges and parsley.

Cocktail Sauce for Seafood

1 cup catsup
¼ cup prepared horseradish, cream style
2 tablespoons lemon juice
½ teaspoon Tabasco sauce
½ teaspoon Worcestershire sauce

Mix all ingredients. Taste. If you prefer a sharper sauce, add more horseradish. Chill.

Seafood

Tartar Sauce

1 cup mayonnaise
1½ tablespoons grated onion and juice
3 tablespoons grated dill pickles
⅛ teaspoon garlic powder
½ teaspoon Worcestershire sauce
⅛ teaspoon Tabasco sauce
1 teaspoon lemon juice

In a medium bowl, blend all ingredients. Let chill at least 2 hours before serving.

Remoulade Sauce

4 tablespoons horseradish mustard
½ cup vinegar
2 tablespoons tomato catsup
1 tablespoon paprika
1 teaspoon salt
1 clove garlic
1 cup salad oil
½ cup chopped green onions
½ cup chopped celery
½ teaspoon cayenne pepper

Place all ingredients into a blender or food processor and blend thoroughly. It should not have any lumps.

Shrimp Remoulade

Marinate boiled, shelled shrimp (see "Boiled Shrimp") in sauce for 4 hours. Serve shrimp and sauce on a bed of lettuce. Wonderful as an appetizer or as a main course.

Shrimp are graded by count per pound: jumbo (15-20), large (20-25), medium (25-35), and small (35-45).

Spices, Accompaniments, etc.
SECTION VII

Cemeteries

The cemeteries are a striking feature of New Orleans, where a high water-table and limited land made in-ground burial impractical. Whole families are interred together in many of the tombs. The remains of the previous burial are pushed to the back to make room for the next one.

SPICES, ACCOMPANIMENTS, ETC.

Roux is made of equal parts of grease or fat and flour, cooked very slowly, with constant stirring, in a heavy pot, until the color is a deep nut-brown. It takes a while to make a *roux*. The trick is to get the flour as dark as possible without burning it. If little black specks appear, some of the flour has burned. You should throw it out, wash out the pot, and start over. Otherwise, the gumbo will have a scorched taste. Often, the chopped vegetables are added immediately to the finished *roux* to stop the cooking by lowering the temperature.

Microwave Roux

1 cup flour
1 cup oil
1 cup chopped onions
½ cup chopped celery
¼ cup chopped bell pepper
3 cloves garlic, minced
¼ cup chopped parsley

Combine flour and oil in 2-quart bowl or deep casserole. Microwave on high for 8 to 9 minutes. Stir at 2 minutes. Roux will be light brown at this time and will take from 30 seconds to 2 minutes to reach the desired dark brown color. Stir again at 1 minute and check color. If further time is needed, check and stir at 30-second intervals. Stir at end of cooking.

Add remaining ingredients and microwave on high for 5 minutes. Stir at 3 minutes and at end of cooking time. Vegetables should be soft, but not brown. If any oil has risen to the top, pour it off.

Roux freezes very well. Freeze in ½-cup amounts for future use.

Oyster Sauce (An accompaniment for turkey or game)

1 pint fresh oysters
½ cup catsup
¼ cup Worcestershire sauce
3 teaspoons prepared mustard
a few drops of Tabasco sauce — to taste

Place oysters with liquor into a pan. Cook over low heat until edges of oysters curl. Cool in refrigerator. Drain oysters and mash them with a fork. Mix all ingredients together thoroughly. Chill until serving time.
NOTE: 2 8-ounce cans of oysters may be substituted for fresh oysters. Omit cooking.

Creole Seasoning Blend

¼ cup salt
¼ cup onion powder
¼ cup garlic powder
2 tablespoons paprika
1 tablespoon cayenne pepper
1 tablespoon black pepper
1½ teaspoons chili powder
1 teaspoon celery seed

Put all ingredients in bowl of food processor and "pulse" until well blended. Cayenne pepper amount may be adjusted for hotter or milder blend. Yield, 1 cup.
NOTE: Eliminate salt to add spice to a salt-free diet. Excellent on any meat or adds zest to vegetables.

Cajun Rice

¼ cup bacon grease
1½ cups raw rice
¾ pound beef ground round
¼ pound ground pork
1 large onion, chopped
3 ribs celery, chopped
1 bell pepper, chopped
¼ teaspoon garlic powder
½ teaspoon thyme
¼ cup chopped parsley
¼ cup chopped green onion
3 teaspoons salt
¼ teaspoon Tabasco
1 bay leaf
1 14½-ounce can whole tomatoes
1 6-ounce can tomato paste
1 cup water

Cook meat in bacon grease until lightly browned, stirring constantly. Add onion, celery and bell pepper and cook until onions are transparent, stirring constantly. Remove from fire, add all other ingredients. Pour into a 9″×13″ baking pan. Bake, covered, in a preheated oven at 350°F for 45 minutes to 1 hour, or until rice is tender.

Louisiana Dirty Rice

4-6 chicken gizzards
4-6 chicken livers
1 pound ground beef
1 pound ground pork
¼ cup flour
3 large onions, chopped
2 bell peppers, chopped
4 stalks celery, chopped
4 cloves garlic, pressed
Few drops Tabasco sauce
Salt and red pepper
10 cups cooked rice
1 cup chopped green onion tops
½ cup chopped parsley

Cook chicken gizzards and livers until tender. Drain, reserving broth. Dice meat and set aside. In heavy iron Dutch oven, fry pork and beef until browned. Remove from pot and in fat remaining, brown flour until very dark brown. Add chopped onions, bell pepper and celery and cook until all are soft and browned. Add garlic, seasoning and reserved broth. Let simmer for about 20 minutes. Add cooked rice and meat, mixing thoroughly. Turn on very low heat, cover and let steam for 30 minutes. Before serving time, add green onion tops and parsley, lifting and blending with a fork. Serves 12.
NOTE: If you like the flavor of liver, increase grizzards and livers to 12 each and decrease ground pork to ½ pound.

Sherried Orange Rice

1 cup raw rice
1 teaspoon salt
½ teaspoon thyme
½ cup minced onion
½ cup seedless raisins
1 medium unpeeled orange, sliced and quartered
1 10½-ounce can chicken broth
6 tablespoons orange juice
⅓ cup dry sherry

In a greased 2-quart casserole, combine rice, seasonings, onion, raisins and orange slices. Bring chicken broth, orange juice and sherry to a boil. Pour over rice mixture, stir once. Cover and bake in a preheated 350°F oven about 45 minutes. Serve with pork or chicken. Serves 6.

Spices, Accompaniments, etc.

Green Rice

2 cups long grain rice
⅔ cup chopped bell pepper
1 cup chopped green onions
⅓ cup minced parsley
2 tablespoons corn oil
1 teaspoon salt
1½ tablespoons Worcestershire sauce
¼ teaspoon red pepper
4 cups chicken bouillon*

Combine all ingredients in a 2-quart casserole. Cover. Bake at 350°F for 75 minutes or until done. Remove cover and toss, as seasonings stay on top.

*If making your bouillon with cubes, use 6 cubes to 4 cups of water

Seasoned Rice

2 cups water
1 tablespoon butter or margarine
1 teaspoon Creole seasoning
¾ teaspoon paprika
1 teaspoon bell pepper flakes
1 teaspoon parsley flakes
¾ teaspoon celery flakes
1 teaspoon granulated chicken bouillon
or 1 chicken bouillon cube
1 cup long grain rice

In a two-quart sauce pan, bring the water to a boil. Add the butter and other seasonings. Add rice and return to boil. Stir and cover. Reduce heat to simmer. Cook for 20 minutes without peeking, or until all the water is absorbed. Stir before serving.

Hard water has a tendency to discolor the rice. To correct this add 1 tablespoon vinegar, 1 teaspoon lemon juice, or ½ teaspoon cream of tartar.

Rice Dressing for Stuffing Turkey

½ cup white wine
1 cup raisins
6 tablespoons butter
1½ cups chopped onion
1½ cups chopped celery
1 medium apple, unpeeled, chopped (1½ cups)
5 cups cooked rice, salted (1¼ cups raw long grain rice)
1 cup seasoned croutons
1½ teaspoons poultry seasoning
1 teaspoon salt

Pour wine over raisins and let stand for 30 minutes. Sauté onions and celery in butter. Combine remaining ingredients. Makes approximately 10 cups.

Oyster Dressing for Poultry

¼ cup butter
½ pound lean ground meat
2 large onions, chopped
5 dozen fresh oysters, cut in half
1 or 2 minced jalapeno peppers (optional)
1½ bunches of green onions, minced
5 slices bread, cubed
Italian bread crumbs
Salt
Garlic powder
Lemon pepper
1 egg (2 if necessary)

Cook oysters over low heat in liquid until they curl. Sauté meat and onions in butter until cooked down. Add oysters, peppers and green onions. Stir and cook for a few minutes, then add bread and enough bread crumbs to absorb juices. Season with salt, garlic powder, and lemon pepper. Stir in one egg. Cook for a few minutes, stirring, and if the dressing is not stiff enough, add another egg. Use as stuffing, or bake in a dish at 350°F for about 30 minutes or until top begins to brown.

Spices, Accompaniments, etc.

Cheese and Grits Casserole

1 cup quick grits
1 teaspoon salt
3 cups boiling water
½ cup butter
8 ounces New York sharp cheddar cheese, grated or cubed
2 eggs, beaten
½ cup milk

Stir grits into boiling, salted water. Add butter and cheese. Cook until blended. Add eggs and milk. Put in a one-quart greased casserole. Bake at 325°F for 25 minutes or until top begins to brown.

Potatoes au Gratin

8 large potatoes, peeled and sliced
2 slices onion
2 tablespoons flour
2 tablespoons margarine
1½ cups milk
½ teaspoon dry mustard
1 teaspoon salt
¼ teaspoon pepper
2 tablespoons margarine
½ cup dry bread crumbs
½ cup grated cheddar cheese

Parboil potatoes and onion in small amount of salted water for 3 minutes. Drain. Place in a 2-quart baking dish. Make a thin white sauce with margarine, flour and milk. Add mustard, salt and pepper. Pour over the potatoes. Melt margarine in sauce pan. Add bread crumbs and cheese. Mix thoroughly. Sprinkle over the potatoes. Bake at 350°F for 30 minutes.

Eggs separate better when they are cold.

Hollandaise Sauce

3 egg yolks
1½ tablespoons lemon juice
¼ teaspoon salt
Dash of paprika
Dash of Tabasco sauce
½ cup butter, melted

Place all of the ingredients in a blender and process on low speed until thick. Transfer to a heat-proof jar, cover the jar, and refrigerate. Before serving, place the jar in a small saucepan with ½ cup water and heat over low heat until desired consistency is obtained. Makes ¾ cup.

Eggs Sardou

4 artichoke bottoms
2 tablespoons butter
2 tablespoons flour
1 cup half-and-half
1 10-ounce package of frozen chopped spinach, cooked and drained
4 tablespoons grated Parmesan cheese
Salt and pepper to taste
4 eggs, poached
¾ cup Hollandaise Sauce
Paprika

Place artichoke bottoms in a greased baking dish. In a small sauce pan melt the butter. Blend in the flour, stirring constantly. Gradually pour in the cream and cook until thickened. Combine the spinach, cheese, salt and pepper, add to the cream sauce, and mix well. Place ¼ of the spinach mixture on each artichoke bottom and keep them warm in the oven. Poach the eggs and place 1 egg on each filled artichoke bottom. Serve the eggs immediately topped with the Hollandaise sauce and sprinkled with paprika. The Hollandaise sauce may be kept warm by placing the blender jar in warm water. Serves 2.

Eggs will beat to a greater volume if at room temperature.

Spices, Accompaniments, etc.

Eggs Benedict

6 toasted English muffin halves	
3 tablespoons butter	
6 slices boiled ham	
¾ cup Hollandaise sauce	
6 eggs	
Paprika	

On individual serving plates, place one English muffin half. Place slice of ham on each. Top with a poached egg. Cover with Hollandaise sauce and sprinkle with paprika. Serves 6.

Vegetable Stir Fry

1 8-ounce package of Neufchatel cheese, cubed
¼ cup sesame seed, toasted
2 cups diagonally cut carrot slices
2 cups diagonally cut celery slices
1 cup thin green pepper strips
2 tablespoons margarine
¼ teaspoon salt
Dash of pepper

Cover cheese cubes with sesame seed, chill. In a skillet, fry vegetables in margarine until crisp tender. Season with salt and pepper. Add cheese to vegetables. Mix lightly. Serves 6 to 8.

Microwave Fig Preserves

2 quarts fresh figs
1 quart sugar
2 whole lemons, sliced thin and seeded

Wash the figs. Place figs, sugar, and lemon slices into a four-quart casserole dish and mix. Cook on high in a 700 watt microwave oven for 50 minutes, stirring every 15 minutes. Pour into scalded jars and seal. Juice will continue to thicken during cooling. Makes 3 pints.

Desserts

CAJUN HOUSE BOAT

The house boat was a practical dwelling in the Louisiana swamps. This one forms part of the Louisiana Swamp Exhibit in the Audubon Zoo.

DESERTS

DESERTS

Pies (cont'd):

Miscellaneous:

Desserts

Napoleon Squares

CRUMB MIXTURE:

¾ cup butter

¼ cup sugar

¼ cup cocoa

1 teaspoon vanilla

2 cups graham cracker crumbs

1 egg, beaten

FILLING:

2 cups confectioners' sugar

¼ cup butter, softened

2 4-ounce cups prepared vanilla pudding

3 tablespoons milk

GLAZE:

1 6-ounce package semi-sweet chocolate chips

2 tablespoons butter

In a 2-quart saucepan combine butter, sugar, cocoa, and vanilla. Cook over medium heat, stirring occasionally, until butter melts — 5 to 6 minutes. Remove from heat. Stir in crumbs and egg. Press on the bottom of a buttered 9″ square pan. Cool.

In a small bowl of the electric mixer, combine all filling ingredients. Beat at medium speed until smooth. Spread over crust, chill until firm (about 30 minutes).

In a quart saucepan melt glaze ingredients over low heat. Spread over bars. Cover, refrigerate until firm (about 1 hour). Cut into squares. Keep refrigerated until ready to serve. Serve in small cupcake papers.

Turtle Bars

1 cup brown sugar

2 cups flour

½ cup margarine

1 cup chopped pecans

⅓ cup margarine

⅔ cup brown sugar

½ teaspoon vanilla

2 cups chocolate chips

Mix 1 cup brown sugar, flour, and ½ cup margarine in a mixer until like a fine meal. Press into a greased 9×13 inch pan. Sprinkle with pecans. Heat together ⅓ cup margarine and ⅔ cup brown sugar; add vanilla, mix well and pour over ingredients already in pan. Bake in a preheated 350°F oven for 20 to 25 minutes, until bottom layer is set; top will not be set. Remove from oven. Sprinkle chocolate chips evenly over top. Let sit a short time, until chips soften, then use back of a spoon to spread the chocolate. After a few minutes, cut into bars but leave in pan to completely cool and hardened.

Cheesecake Bars

2 cups flour
1½ cups packed brown sugar
1 cup cold butter
1½ cups quick-cooking oats
2 8-ounce packages cream cheese
½ cup sugar
3 eggs
¼ cup milk
1 teaspoon vanilla
¼ cup lemon juice

In large bowl combine flour and brown sugar; cut in butter until mixture is crumbly. Stir in oats. Reserve 1½ cups of the oat and flour mixture for top of cake; press the remaining oat mixture into the bottom of a greased 15×10 inch jelly roll pan. Bake 10 minutes in a preheated 350°F oven. In a medium bowl beat cream cheese and sugar until fluffy. Add eggs, milk and vanilla. Mix well. Add lemon juice. Mix and pour over crust. Sprinkle with reserved oat mixture. Return to oven, bake 25 to 30 minutes at 350°F. When cool cut in squares. Store in refrigerator.

Praline Cookies

1 box graham crackers
1 cup margarine
1 cup light brown sugar
¾ cup chopped pecans
1 teaspoon salt
1½ ounces semi-sweet chocolate, melted and cooled.

In a buttered jellyroll pan arrange the graham crackers in one layer (you will not use the entire box). They should be close, but not overlapping.

In a small saucepan, melt the butter and brown sugar and boil for 1 minute. Add the chopped pecans and boil 1 minute more. Pour this mixture over graham crackers as evenly as possible. Bake in a preheated 350°F oven for 10 minutes and remove from oven. Cut into squares while still warm and soft, but not runny. Drizzle the chocolate evenly over the top of the praline. If the praline sets too quickly, put the pan back into the oven. Cook only one batch at a time.

Desserts

Oatmeal Cookies

1 cup vegetable shortening
1 cup brown sugar
1 teaspoon baking soda
2 tablespoons cold water
½ teaspoon salt
1 teaspoon vanilla extract
1 cup flour
2 cups quick-cooking oatmeal
1 cup chopped pecans (optional)

Cream shortening and brown sugar well. Mix baking soda and cold water and stir into the creamed mixture. Stir in salt and vanilla extract. Stir in flour, then oatmeal and pecans. Shape rounded teaspoons full into balls and place on greased cookie sheets. Press to flatten with a greased glass. Bake in a preheated 350°F oven for 8 minutes or until cookies are lightly browned.

Oatmeal Chocolate Chip Chocolate Cookies

1 cup shortening
¾ cup sugar
¾ cup brown sugar
2 eggs
1 teaspoon vanilla
1½ cups flour
¼ cup cocoa
½ teaspoon salt
1 teaspoon baking soda
1 tablespoon hot water
2 cups quick-cooking oatmeal
1 cup chopped pecans (optional)
2 cups (12-ounce bag) chocolate chips

Cream shortening and sugars together. Add eggs, one at a time, beating well after each. Add vanilla and mix. Sift flour, cocoa, salt and baking soda together and mix into creamed mixture. Stir in hot water, then stir in oatmeal, pecans, and chocolate chips. Drop by heaping teaspoons onto greased cookie sheets. Bake in a preheated 350°F oven for 10-12 minutes or until cookies are lightly browned.

Darlene's Angel Cloud Cookies

1 cup butter (room temperature)
½ cup sugar
2 cups sifted flour
1 teaspoon vanilla
½ cup coconut flakes
Confectioners sugar

Cream butter and sugar. Gradually add flour, coconut and vanilla and blend well. Roll gently by hand into small balls (about 1 teaspoon each) and place on ungreased cookie sheets. Flatten ball slightly with a fork dipped in cold water. Bake in a preheated 350°F oven for 15 to 20 minutes. Dust cookies with confectioners sugar and cool. Makes 4 dozen.

Easy Pralines

1 3½-ounce package vanilla pudding mix (not instant)
1 cup white sugar
½ cup dark brown sugar
½ cup evaporated milk
1 tablespoon butter
1-2 cups pecan halves

Combine first 5 ingredients and stir to rolling boil, then cook slowly for 3-5 minutes. Take off heat and stir in pecan halves. Beat until thickened. Drop by spoonfuls on waxed paper. Let cool. Wrap in plastic wrap. If it gets too hard while beating, add a little more evaporated milk; if too soft, beat a little longer. For a variation, use chocolate pudding instead of vanilla.

Pralines

1 cup evaporated milk
1 cup light brown sugar
1 cup granulated sugar
1 tablespoon butter
1 teaspoon vanilla
1½ cups pecans

Put milk and sugars in heavy pot, mix well, and cook until it reaches "soft ball" stage (234°F). Remove from heat and add rest of ingredients. Beat until cool and slightly thickened, then spoon onto waxed paper. Makes 1½ to 2 dozen.
NOTE: Stirring while cooking will produce a sugary texture.

Pralines a l'Orleans (Microwave)

1 cup whipping cream
1 pound light brown sugar
2 cups pecan halves
2 tablespoons margarine

Mix cream and brown sugar together in a 4-quart bowl. Microwave on high (100%) for 13 minutes (stirring not necessary). Candy thermometer reading should be 234°F (soft ball stage). Quickly add pecans and margarine, stirring to mix. Drop candy by teaspoons onto a sheet of foil. Let cool for at least an hour.

Bananas Foster Pralines

1 cup sugar
1 cup dark brown sugar
2 tablespoons light corn syrup
½ cup half-and-half
2 tablespoons butter
1 teaspoon vanilla
2 tablespoons rum (preferably dark)
3 tablespoons banana liqueur
1 cup pecan halves or pieces

In a saucepan dissolve the sugars and syrup in the cream over medium heat. Bring the mixture to a boil and continue cooking until a candy thermometer registers 228°F, stirring occasionally. Add butter, vanilla, rum, liqueur and pecans and cook to 236°F (soft ball stage) and remove from heat. Cool the candy to 225°F and beat just until thickened. (This happens almost instantly.) Drop the candy by tablespoonsful on waxed paper, working rapidly. The candy will flatten out. When cool, store in covered container. Makes 15 to 20 pralines.

Heavenly Hash Candy

2¼ cups small marshmallows
3 cups sugar
½ cup cocoa
½ cup margarine, melted
1 12-ounce can evaporated milk
2 cups pecans, coarsely chopped
1 7-ounce jar marshmallow creme
1 teaspoon vanilla

Evenly spread marshmallows in the bottom of a 9×12 inch pan that has been thoroughly greased (sides and bottom). Mix sugar and cocoa thoroughly. Gradually add melted margarine and milk. Stir until smooth. Cook on medium heat to soft ball stage (235°F on candy thermometer). Remove from heat. Add pecans, marshmallow creme and vanilla. Place pan in cold water and beat until mixture begins to thicken. Pour mixture over marshmallows in greased pan. Cool thoroughly and cut into squares.

Ultimate Chocolate Cake

3 squares unsweetened chocolate
½ cup butter
2 cups brown sugar (packed)
3 eggs
2 teaspoons vanilla
2¼ cups flour
2 teaspoons baking soda
½ teaspoon salt
1 cup sour cream
1 cup boiling water

Grease and flour two 9-inch cake pans. Melt chocolate over hot but not boiling water. Let cool. In large mixing bowl combine butter and brown sugar. Add eggs and vanilla and beat until fluffy (about 4-5 minutes). Sift together flour, soda, and salt. Add alternately to creamed sugar mixture with sour cream, ending with flour mixture. Add cooled melted chocolate and mix well. Gradually stir in boiling water. Pour into prepared pans and bake in a preheated 350°F oven for 30 to 35 minutes. Check cake with toothpick. When toothpick comes out clean, cake is done. Remove from oven. Let cool in pans for 10 minutes, then turn out onto cake rack to cool completely before frosting with chocolate fudge frosting.

CHOCOLATE FUDGE FROSTING:
4 squares unsweetened chocolate
½ cup butter, softened
1 pound confectioners sugar
2 teaspoons vanilla
4-6 tablespoons milk

Melt chocolate over hot but not boiling water. Let cool to room temperature. In small mixing bowl beat softened butter with sugar and vanilla. Add 4 tablespoons milk and melted chocolate. Beat well, adding the remaining milk if necessary to bring it to spreading consistency. This is enough to ice two 9-inch layers.

Desserts

Pineapple Upside-Down Cake

BATTER:
2 eggs
⅔ cup sugar
6 tablespoons milk
1 teaspoon vanilla
1 cup flour
⅓ teaspoon baking powder
¼ teaspoon salt
TOPPING:
⅓ cup butter (melted)
½ cup brown sugar
1 20-ounce can sliced pineapple, drained
maraschino cherries and pecan halves for decoration

In a medium mixing bowl, beat eggs until fluffy. Gradually add sugar, beating constantly. Add milk and vanilla. Mix well. Sift together the flour, baking powder and salt. Add to the batter, mixing well.

Pour the melted butter into an 8-inch baking pan. Sprinkle the sugar over butter. Arrange pineapple slices on sugar. Decorate with cherries and pecan halves. Pour batter over fruit. Bake in a preheated 350°F oven for 45 minutes. Remove from the oven; invert on a serving plate. Allow the sugar to run down sides of the cake. Serve hot or cold.

Punch Bowl Cake

1 (11½-ounces) pound cake or Angel Food Cake
2 (8-ounce) containers whipped topping
1 (20-ounce) can crushed pineapple, drained
1 (3.4-ounce) package instant vanilla pudding
2 cups milk
1 (21-ounce) can cherry pie filling
1 cup coarsely chopped pecans

In a bowl blend together the milk and the pudding mix for 2 minutes and allow to set. Cut the cake into ¼ inch slices and set aside.

In a punch bowl, layer ½ of the cake, 1 container of whipped topping, ½ of the crushed pineapple, pudding, pie filling and pecans. Repeat for the second layer. Refrigerate at least 3 hours or overnight.

Apple Cake

4 to 5 cups diced cooking apples
2 eggs, beaten
2 cups sugar
2 teaspoons cinnamon
½ cup oil
1 cup coarsely chopped nuts
2 cups flour
2 teaspoons soda
¾ teaspoon salt

Place diced apples in a large bowl. Over these break the eggs and add sugar, cinnamon, oil and nuts. Mix thoroughly with a fork. Sift the remaining dry ingredients together and stir into the apple mixture. Press into a 9×13 inch buttered and floured pan. Bake 55 minutes in a preheated 350°F oven. Delicious served plain or with a lemon sauce.

Poppy Seed Cake

3 cups flour
1½ teaspoons baking powder
¼ teaspoon baking soda
1½ teaspoons salt
1½ tablespoons poppy seeds
2 cups sugar
1½ cups milk
1 cup vegetable oil
3 eggs
1½ teaspoons almond extract
1½ teaspoons vanilla

In a large mixing bowl, combine dry ingredients. Add milk, oil, eggs, almond extract, and vanilla. Mix 2 minutes at medium speed or until well blended. Pour into 2 greased and floured loaf pans. Bake approximately 1 hour and 10 minutes in a preheated 350°F oven, or until toothpick inserted near center comes out clean.

GLAZE:
¾ cup sugar
2 tablespoons butter
¼ cup orange juice
½ teaspoon vanilla
½ teaspoon almond extract

Mix all ingredients in small saucepan. Heat to dissolve sugar and melt butter. Pour over warm cake. Let sit for 5 minutes, then remove from pan.

Bust Your Girdle Cake

1 18½-ounce box yellow cake mix
½ cup margarine, melted
1 egg
8-ounces cream cheese
1 box confectioners sugar
2 eggs
1 teaspoon vanilla
1 20-ounce can cherry pie filling
whipped topping (optional)

Thoroughly combine cake mix, melted margarine and 1 egg. Press into the bottom and slightly up the sides of a 9×13×2 inch oven-proof pan. Mix the cream cheese, confectioners sugar, 2 remaining eggs and vanilla thoroughly. Pour over mixture already in the pan. Bake in a preheated 350°F oven for 35-40 minutes. Cool and spread with cherry pie filling. Chill. You may spread a thin layer of whipped topping over the pie filling if desired.

Pecan Chocolate Torte and Filling

6 eggs, separated
½ teaspoon salt
1 teaspoon vanilla
¾ cup sugar
1 cup sifted flour
1 cup finely-chopped pecans
Chopped pecans for topping

In the large bowl of the electric mixer combine the egg yolks, salt and vanilla, beat until very light and lemon-colored. Beat ½ cup sugar in gradually, continue beating until very light and fluffy (about 5 minutes at medium speed). Stir in flour and the 1 cup of finely-chopped pecans.

Beat egg whites until they form soft peaks; beat in remaining ¼ cup of sugar gradually, beating until glossy. Fold into yolk mixture. Divide batter equally between 3 greased and floured 8 inch layer pans. Spread just enough to level. Bake in a 300°F preheated oven until done, 20 to 25 minutes. Cool pans on a rack 10 minutes; remove torte from pans and cool thoroughly on rack. Put layers together with Chocolate Creme Filling using ⅓ of the filling on each layer. Sprinkle top with chopped pecans. Chill in refrigerator until filling is firm. Scrape excess filling off of torte. Cover the sides of torte with Chocolate Satin Frosting. Chill and serve. Serves 8-10.

CHOCOLATE CREME FILLING:

1 6-ounce package semi-sweet chocolate pieces

¾ cup cold butter or margarine

1¼ cups sifted confectioners sugar

½ teaspoon salt

1 egg

3 teaspoons rum

In the top of a double boiler melt chocolate over boiling water. Cool, stirring often during cooling (chocolate must be cool, but not chilled, when added to butter mixture). In the large bowl of the electric mixer whip butter until fluffy. Mix in sugar and salt, then beat at medium speed until mixture is fluffy and smooth, about 2 minutes. Fold in rum and chocolate. Cool in refrigerator to stiffen slightly before spreading on the torte layers.

CHOCOLATE SATIN FROSTING:

1 cup sugar

¼ cup cornstarch

¼ teaspoon salt

1 cup boiling water

2 squares unsweetened chocolate, melted

3 tablespoons butter or margarine

Combine sugar, cornstarch and salt in a saucepan; mix well. Add water gradually, stirring constantly during addition. Place over low heat and cook until smooth and thickened, stirring constantly. Add chocolate and butter. Continue cooking until smooth and thick. Chill over ice water until thick enough to spread; stir frequently during cooling. Spread sides of torte with frosting.

Have all cake ingredients at room temperature, assemble utensils, prepare pans, and set oven temperature before starting to mix.

Desserts

Strawberry Angel Surprise

1 10-inch round angel food cake
2 cups strawberry ice cream, softened
1½ pints whipping cream, whipped
3 tablespoons sugar
Fresh or frozen strawberries

Cut a 1-inch slice from the top of the cake and set aside. Cut out a ring 2 inches wide and 2 inches deep. Spoon in softened ice cream. Replace the slice cut from top of cake. Frost the top and sides of cake with whipped cream sweetened with sugar. Store in freezer until ready to serve. Approximately 10 minutes before serving, slice, place on dessert plates and garnish with strawberries.

Chocolate Lover's Delight

7 1-ounce squares semi-sweet chocolate
½ cup butter
¾ cup sugar
¼ teaspoon vanilla extract
7 egg yolks
7 egg whites
¼ cup sugar
Chocolate shavings
Sweetened whipped cream

Melt chocolate and butter together over low heat. Place in mixer bowl with ¾ cup sugar, vanilla extract and egg yolks. Beat for 3 minutes on high speed.

In a separate bowl beat the egg whites until soft peaks form. Add remaining ¼ cup sugar slowly, beating constantly until whites hold their peaks. Fold egg white mixture slowly into the chocolate mixture with a spatula. Pour the batter into an ungreased 9 inch springform pan. Bake in a preheated 325°F oven for 40 minutes. Remove torte from oven and let it cool. It will fall. Run knife around edge and remove side of springform pan. Chill until serving time. Garnish with chocolate shavings and whipped cream.

Chocolate Cream Roll

½ cup sifted cake flour
½ teaspoon baking powder
¼ teaspoon salt
2 1-ounce squares unsweetened chocolate
4 eggs, at room temperature
¾ cup sugar
1 teaspoon vanilla extract
2 tablespoons sugar
¼ teaspoon baking soda
3 tablespoons cold water
Granulated sugar
1 cup whipping cream
¼ teaspoon almond extract
½ cup semi-sweet chocolate chips
2 tablespoons butter or margarine

Grease a 15×10×1 inch jelly roll pan. Line bottom with waxed paper. Preheat oven to 375°F.

Sift flour, baking powder and salt and set aside. Melt unsweetened chocolate over hot water and set aside. Break eggs into large bowl of electric mixer. Gradually add ¼ cup sugar to eggs while beating at high speed. Continue beating until mixture is thick and light. Fold in vanilla and flour mixture all at once. Add 2 tablespoons sugar, baking soda and cold water to melted chocolate and stir until thick and light. Quickly fold chocolate mixture into egg mixture. Pour into jelly roll pan and spread evenly. Bake in preheated 375°F oven 15-20 minutes or until cake springs back when gently pressed with finger.

Lay a clean dish towel on a counter and sift a thick layer of granulated sugar over it. When cake is done, run knife around sides to loosen cake, then turn it out onto the sugared cloth. Carefully peel off waxed paper and trim edges of cake. Let cool for five minutes. Then fold end of towel over end of the cake and gently roll the cake up with the towel in it. Carefully lift the rolled cake onto a cake rack to cool thoroughly — for about an hour.

Just before serving, whip the cream, adding sugar and almond extract. Unroll cake and spread whipped cream to within one inch of cake edges. Roll up the cake, lifting end of towel to push it along. Melt semi-sweet chocolate with butter over hot, not boiling, water. Stir to mix well and spread over top of chocolate roll.

Ice Box Cherry Pie For a crowd (makes 3 pies)

1 20-ounce can sour cherries
1 20-ounce can crushed pineapple
4 bananas, sliced
1 cup chopped pecans
7 tablespoons cornstarch
1 teaspoon salt (optional)
1 teaspoon red food coloring
1 teaspoon vanilla extract
1/4 teaspoon almond extract
2 cups sugar
3 8 or 9 inch graham cracker pie shells
3 - 4 cups whipped topping

Drain the cherries and pineapple and reserve the juice. Mix the cherries, pineapple, bananas and pecans together in a bowl. Add enough water to the juice to make 2 cups and pour it into a 4-quart pot. Add the cornstarch, salt, food coloring, extracts and sugar. Cook this mixture, stirring constantly, until it thickens. Stir in the fruit.

Pour into 3 graham cracker pie shells and cool slightly. Spread each pie with a thin layer of whipped topping and refrigerate.

Lemon Chiffon Pie

1 8 or 9 inch graham cracker crumb crust (reserve 1 tablespoon crumbs for garnish)
1 14-ounce can sweetened condensed milk
1/3 cup lemon juice
4 drops yellow food coloring
3 egg whites
1/4 teaspoon cream of tartar
2 cups whipped topping

In a medium bowl combine condensed milk, lemon juice and food coloring. In a small bowl beat the egg whites with cream of tartar until stiff but not dry; gently fold into the sweetened condensed milk mixture. Pour into prepared crust. Chill 3 hours or until set. Top with whipped topping and reserved crumbs. Refrigerate.

Chocolate Sundae Pie

CRUST:

1¼ cups coconut macaroon cookie crumbs

½ cup chopped pecans

¼ cup butter or margarine, melted

Combine crumbs, nuts and butter. Press firmly into the bottom and up the sides of a 9 inch pie pan. Bake in a preheated 350°F oven for 8-10 minutes. Cool.

FILLING:

⅔ cup packed light brown sugar

3 tablespoons flour

2 tablespoons cornstarch

½ teaspoon salt

2¼ cups milk

½ cup chocolate-flavored syrup

3 egg yolks, well beaten

1 teaspoon vanilla

Whipped cream, cherries, chocolate curls for garnish.

Combine sugar, flour, cornstarch and salt in a saucepan. Stir in milk, chocolate syrup and egg yolks. Cook over medium heat, stirring constantly, until mixture boils; then cook and stir one minute longer. Remove from heat; blend in butter and vanilla. Pour into baked pie crust. Place plastic wrap directly on top of filling. Chill. Remove the wrap, and garnish with whipped cream, cherries and chocolate curls if desired.

French Chocolate Pie

½ cup butter

¾ cup sugar

2 squares melted unsweetened chocolate

2 eggs

2 cups thawed whipped topping

1 9-inch pie shell, baked

In small bowl, cream butter and sugar together with electric mixer. Add chocolate. Add eggs, one at a time, beating at high speed for 5 minutes after each addition. Fold in whipped topping. Pour into baked pie shell. Chill until firm, about 2 hours, or freeze.

Chocolate Coffee Pie

PASTRY:
1¼ cups flour, unsifted
5 tablespoons butter
¼ cup brown sugar, firmly packed
¾ cup finely chopped pecans
1 1-ounce square unsweetened chocolate, grated
1 teaspoon vanilla
1 scant tablespoon water

Preheat oven to 350°F. Place flour, butter, and sugar in food processor. Pulse until well blended. Add pecans, chocolate, vanilla, and water. Pulse just until a ball of dough is formed. Butter a 10-inch pie plate and turn mixture into the plate, pressing into the bottom and sides with the back of a spoon. Bake for 15 minutes. Cool.

FILLING:
¾ cup butter, softened
1 cup sugar
1½-ounces unsweetened chocolate, melted
1 tablespoon instant coffee
3 eggs

Beat butter until creamy. Gradually add sugar, beating until light and lemon-colored. Melt chocolate over hot water, cool slightly, and add to butter mixture. Then stir in instant coffee. Add eggs one at a time, beating well after each addition. Pour filling into the cooled pie shell and refrigerate, covered, overnight.

COFFEE TOPPING:
2 cups heavy cream
½ cup powdered sugar
2 tablespoons instant coffee
2 tablespoons coffee liqueur
Chocolate curls for garnish

Beat cream until stiff, then add powdered sugar, coffee, and liqueur. Spread over filling and garnish with chocolate curls. Refrigerate for at least 2 hours before serving. Serves 10.

Cajun Custard Pie

4 cups cream
3 eggs
1 ¼ cups sugar
2 tablespoons cornstarch
2 tablespoons vanilla
¼ cup melted butter
Dash of cinnamon
Dash of nutmeg
2 9-inch pie shells, unbaked

In a heavy metal saucepan heat cream and scald. In a large bowl combine eggs, sugar and cornstarch and beat until creamy. Add vanilla, butter, cinnamon and nutmeg. Continue beating until all ingredients are well blended. Gradually mix one cup of hot cream into the egg mixture, stirring constantly. Blend well. Now pour the egg mixture into the remaining hot cream, continuing to stir. Remove from heat and allow to cool slightly. Pour the filling into a pie shell. Cut the remaining dough into ½-inch strips; arrange the strips in a lattice across the top of the pie. Bake in a preheated 350°F oven for 45 minutes or until golden brown on top.

Pecan Pie

1 ½ cups dark corn syrup
½ cup sugar
1 tablespoon butter
3 eggs, beaten
1 tablespoon vanilla
1 cup pecans
Unbaked pie shell

Combine syrup and sugar in a saucepan. Heat to dissolve sugar. Add butter. Let cool to lukewarm and add beaten eggs, vanilla, and pecans. Pour into unbaked pie shell. Bake in preheated oven at 350° to 375°F for 25 to 30 minutes or until set.

Shiny metal or heatproof glass pans are preferred for cake baking because they reflect heat away from the cake, producing a tender crust. When using glass pans, reduce the oven temperature 25°F.

Desserts

Pecan and Fig Pie

(Figs are plentiful and often canned in Cajun homes.)

1 tablespoon cornstarch
¼ cup sugar
¾ cup corn syrup
½ cup cane syrup
1 teaspoon vanilla
3 eggs, beaten
1 cup chopped pecans
½ cup mashed canned figs or fig preserves
Dash of cinnamon
Dash of nutmeg
1 9-inch unbaked pie shell

Combine cornstarch and sugar, add syrups, vanilla and eggs; blend well. Add nuts and figs and mix again. Add cinnamon and nutmeg and stir into mixture. Pour into unbaked pie shell and bake in a preheated 325°F oven for 45 minutes.

Luscious Pecan Pie

9-inch unbaked pie shell
3 eggs
⅔ cup sugar
⅓ teaspoon salt
⅓ cup melted margarine
1 cup dark corn syrup
1 cup pecan halves

Beat eggs, then add sugar, salt, margarine and syrup, beating well after each addition. Mix in pecan halves. Pour into unbaked pie shell. Bake in preheated oven until set and pastry is nicely browned, 40 to 50 minutes at 375°F. Cool.

Heavy metal pots are best for cooking candy, because the syrup will not stick as easily as in thin ones.

Louisiana Yam Pie

3 eggs, beaten
3 tablespoons butter, melted
1/2 teaspoon salt
3/4 cup brown sugar, packed
1 teaspoon cinnamon
1/2 teaspoon nutmeg
1 teaspoon vanilla
2 cups mashed cooked yams
1 cup canned evaporated milk
9-inch unbaked pie shell
Pecans, whipped cream or topping for garnish

Combine beaten eggs, butter, salt, sugar, spices, vanilla, and yams. Beat until well blended. Add milk, mix well, and pour into unbaked pie shell. Bake in preheated 375°F oven for 1 hour or until knife inserted near center comes out clean. Remove from oven and garnish with pecans. When thoroughly cooled, pie may be topped with whipped cream or low calorie topping before serving.

Mile High Strawberry Pie

1 9-inch pie shell, baked
2 egg whites
1 10-ounce package frozen strawberries, thawed
1 cup sugar
1 teaspoon lemon juice
1/2 pint whipping cream, whipped

Beat egg whites until fluffy; add strawberries, sugar, and lemon juice. Beat at high speed 10 minutes. Fold in whipped cream. Pour into baked pie shell and freeze. Serve frozen; cut with a knife dipped in warm water. You can use a crumb crust.
NOTE: 1 cup of whipped topping may be substituted for whipped cream; reduce sugar to 3/4 cup.

Desserts

Bananas Foster

1 tablespoon butter
2 tablespoons brown sugar
1 ripe banana, peeled, sliced lengthwise and halved
Dash cinnamon
1 tablespoon banana liqueur
1 ounce white rum
1 ounce brandy
Vanilla ice cream

Melt butter in chafing dish. Add brown sugar and blend well. Add banana pieces and sauté until they are tender to the touch. Sprinkle with cinnamon. Let simmer for a minute or two. Combine banana liqueur with rum and brandy and heat. Ignite, basting banana with flaming liquid. When flame dies out, serve over vanilla ice cream. Serves 2.
NOTE: Mixture must be hot to flame.

Caramel Custard

¾ cup sugar
1 can (14-ounce) sweetened condensed milk
1 cup milk
3 eggs
2 egg yolks
1½ teaspoons vanilla

Heat sugar in skillet over low heat until sugar is melted and turns a deep caramel color. Remove from heat and immediately divide into six custard cups. Turn cups to evenly coat the sides and bottom. Combine remaining ingredients in food processor or blender for 10-12 seconds. Pour into prepared cups. Place custard cups in 9×13 inch pan with one inch of hot water. Bake in a preheated 350°F oven for 45-50 minutes. Serve in cups or turn out on serving plates.

Test bread puddings and baked custards for doneness with a silver knife. Insert the knife in the center and if it comes out clean, it's ready.

Lemon Sauce

1 tablespoon butter
½ cup sugar
1 egg, well beaten
2 tablespoons cornstarch dissolved in 2 tablespoons water
2 cups boiling water
Juice and grated zest of one lemon

Beat the butter and sugar until creamy. Put into a saucepan; add the well beaten egg and dissolved cornstarch. Mix well. Slowly add the boiling water, stirring constantly, and cook, continuing to stir, until thickened. Remove from heat. Add the lemon juice and grated zest. This is wonderful served warm or cold over bread pudding.

Bread Pudding

Louisianians love bread — but not *stale* bread. However, they don't throw stale bread away. They 'revive' it in the oven, or make something from it. Bread pudding is a favorite. All recipes for it call for butter, sugar, eggs, and milk. Beyond that, different cooks do different things, most good, and all different. It is often served with rum or whiskey sauce.

Custard Bread Pudding

6 jumbo eggs
3 cups sugar
1 12-ounce can evaporated milk
4¼ cups milk
9 slices medium-toasted buttered bread
3 tablespoons vanilla
1 tablespoon cinnamon
1 teaspoon nutmeg
Raisins (optional)

Preheat oven to 325°F. Beat eggs and sugar. Scald milk. Break buttered toast into small pieces and put in 9×13 inch baking dish. Add eggs, sugar, vanilla, cinnamon, and nutmeg to scalded milk. If desired, sprinkle raisins on top of toast. Pour milk mixture over toasted bread and stir. Let sit 5 minutes. Sprinkle cinnamon and nutmeg on top. Bake for 1 hour or until knife inserted near center comes out clean. NOTE: This is also delicious when only 2 cups of sugar are used.

Bananas Foster Bread Pudding

1 12-ounce loaf stale French bread, broken in small pieces (or 9-11 cups any type stale bread)
1 cup milk
4 cups half-and-half
2½ cups sugar
8 tablespoons butter, melted
4 eggs
2 tablespoons vanilla
3 sliced bananas

Combine all ingredients; mixture should be very moist but not soupy. Pour into buttered 9×13 inch baking dish. Place on middle rack of cold oven. Bake in a 350°F oven for approximately 1 hour and 15 minutes until top is golden brown. Serve warm with bananas foster sauce.

BANANAS FOSTER SAUCE:
½ cup butter
2 cups dark brown sugar
4 ounces dark rum
2 ounces banana liqueur
2 bananas cut in small pieces

Melt butter and add brown sugar to form a creamy paste. Stir in liquors until smooth sauce is formed. Add bananas and simmer for 2 minutes. Serve warm over warm bread pudding.

COLD WATER TEST FOR CANDY OR ICING:
Use a fresh cup of cold water for each sample. Drop 1 teaspoon of syrup into the water. Shape it into a ball to test the degree of doneness.

Soft ball: Can be picked up but flattens
Firm ball: Holds its shape until pressed.
Hard ball: Holds its shape but is pliable.
Soft crack: Separates into hard but not brittle threads.
Hard crack: Separates into hard brittle threads.

Traditional Bread Pudding

1 12-ounce loaf stale French bread, crumbled
(or 6-8 cups any type stale bread)
3 cups milk
2½ cups sugar
5 tablespoons butter, melted
4 eggs
2 cups half-and-half
2 tablespoons vanilla
1 cup raisins
1 cup coconut
1 cup chopped pecans
1 teaspoon cinnamon
1 teaspoon nutmeg

Combine all ingredients; mixture should be very moist but not soupy. Pour into buttered 9×14 inch baking dish. Place in cold oven. Bake in a 350°F oven for approximately 1 hour and 15 minutes until top is golden brown and knife inserted near center comes out clean. Serve warm with Lemon, Custard or Hard sauce.

CUSTARD SAUCE:
2 cups milk
⅔ cup sugar
4 eggs
1 teaspoon vanilla

In top of double boiler, beat the eggs and sugar until light and creamy; add milk and vanilla. Using a double boiler, cook over simmering (not boiling) water, stirring constantly, until the sauce starts to thicken. Cooking too long will cause the sauce to curdle. Remove from heat. Chill, and serve over bread pudding.

HARD SAUCE:
¼ cup butter or margarine
1 cup sugar
2 egg whites
1 teaspoon vanilla

Beat the butter and sugar until creamy. Beat the egg whites until stiff, then slowly add to the sugar and butter. Add the vanilla. Serve on bread pudding or cooked fruit desserts.

Desserts

Strawberry Parfait

1 pint vanilla ice cream
1 cup whipped cream
9 tablespoons Cointreau liqueur
1 quart fresh strawberries, mashed
½ cup confectioners sugar

In the large bowl of the electric mixer whip ice cream until creamy and fold in whipped cream. Add 6 tablespoons Cointreau. Combine strawberries, sugar, and remaining liqueur. Blend into ice cream mixture. Serve in chilled parfait glasses. Serves 6.

Orleans Apple Torte

PASTRY:
⅓ cup sugar
⅓ cup butter
1 tablespoon shortening
¼ teaspoon vanilla
⅛ teaspoon salt
1 cup flour

Cream together sugar, butter, and shortening. Add vanilla, salt, and flour. Blend well. Pat into the bottom and ½ inch up the sides of a lightly greased 9 inch spring-form pan.

TORTE:
4-5 Winesap apples
8 ounces cream cheese, softened
¼ cup sugar
1 egg
½ teaspoon grated lemon peel
⅛ teaspoon salt
¼ teaspoon vanilla
Cinnamon and sugar
¼ cup sliced almonds

Pare, core and slice apples to measure 4 cups. Place apples in a shallow pan. Cover with foil and bake in a preheated 400°F oven for 15 minutes while preparing filling. Beat cream cheese and sugar together. Add egg, lemon peel, salt, and vanilla. Beat until smooth. Pour into prepared pastry crust. Top with partially cooked apple slices. Sprinkle with cinnamon, sugar and almonds. Bake at 400°F for about 40 minutes until apples are lightly browned. Cool well before cutting.

English Toffee Torte

6 ounces vanilla wafers
1 cup pecans
½ cup melted butter (not margarine)
1 cup confectioners' sugar
½ cup melted butter
1½ squares melted chocolate
3 egg yolks, well beaten
3 egg whites, well beaten
1 teaspoon vanilla

Grind together vanilla wafers and pecans. Add ½ cup melted butter and confectioners' sugar. Mix until crumbly; set aside. Mix melted butter and chocolate in mixing bowl. Add well-beaten egg yolks, mix well and allow to cool. Fold in beaten egg whites and vanilla. Grease 8-inch square pan and line with half of the crumb mixture. Spread with cooled chocolate mixture and cover with remaining crumb mixture. Store in refrigerator from 6 hours to overnight. Cut in squares to serve.

Lemon Tarts

CRUST:
1½ cups flour
10 tablespoons margarine
3 tablespoons water

In a food processor mix flour and margarine until crumbly. Add water until dough forms a ball. Pat dough into individual tart pans. Prick dough and bake at 425°F for 8 minutes.

FILLING:
½ cup lemon juice
1 teaspoon lemon rind
2 cups sugar
¾ cup margarine
5 eggs, well beaten

In a double boiler combine juice, rind and sugar. Add margarine and heat over boiling water until margarine is melted. Stir in eggs. Cook, stirring, until mixture thickens enough to pile up slightly. Cool. Spoon into shells. The filling will keep several weeks in the refrigerator. Makes 4 dozen tarts.

Baked Alaska Cheese Cake

1 7-ounce package flaked coconut, toasted
¼ cup chopped pecans
3 tablespoons margarine, melted
2 8-ounce packages cream cheese, softened
⅓ cup sugar
3 tablespoons cocoa
2 tablespoons water
1 teaspoon vanilla
3 eggs, separated
Dash salt
1 7-ounce jar marshmallow creme
½ cup chopped pecans

In a small bowl combine coconut, pecans and margarine. Press this mixture into the bottom of a 9 inch springform pan.

In the large bowl of an electric mixer, combine the cream cheese, sugar, cocoa, water and vanilla at medium speed until well blended. Blend in egg yolks and pour over crust. Bake in a preheated oven 350°F for 30 minutes. Loosen cake from rim of pan, cool before removing rim of pan.

Beat egg whites and salt until foamy, gradually add marshmallow creme. Continue beating until stiff peaks form. Sprinkle pecans over cheesecake to within ½ inch of outer edge. Spread marshmallow creme mixture over top of cheesecake to seal. Brown in preheated 350°F oven for 15 minutes. Serves 12.

Chess Squares

1 18½-ounce box yellow cake mix
½ cup butter, melted
1 egg
1 cup chopped pecans
1 1-pound box confectioners' sugar
1 8-ounce package cream cheese
3 eggs

In a large bowl mix together by hand the cake mix, ½ cup butter, 1 egg and 1 cup chopped pecans. Press the mixture into a greased 11"×13" baking dish. In the large bowl of the electric mixer blend the sugar, cream cheese and 3 eggs and pour the mixture over the pressed cake batter. Bake the cake in a 325°F preheated oven for 1 hour. Cut into squares before completely cool. Makes 3 dozen squares.

Flamed Louisiana Peaches

4 ripe fresh peaches, sliced
¼ cup butter
3 tablespoons Amaretto liqueur
3 tablespoons rum
Vanilla ice cream

In a chafing dish sauté peaches in butter. Add Amaretto and blend well. Heat rum in a small saucepan. Ignite and pour over peaches. Serve over vanilla ice cream. Serves 6. NOTE: Heat liqueur in a small pan with a long handle. Take care to heat until just under boiling point. Heating too much or for too long will evaporate the alcohol. The secret lies in having the food and the liqueur at the proper temperature before flaming.

Bakeries

Delicious home-made bread, pies, cakes, and other good things are part of almost everyone's idea of the past. In many parts of America that's an accurate picture, but not in New Orleans! New Orleans retained the European custom of buying many things from the bakery, especially bread and fancy desserts. Economy was one reason. Old-fashioned brick ovens were heated by building a large fire inside, raking out the coals, and baking in the stored heat. It was wasteful to bake only one or two things. Heat, in sub-tropical New Orleans, was another reason. As a result, people who baked at home made large quantities, and their baked-goods went stale. On the other hand, what you bought from the bakery was usually fresh. People tended to restrict home-baking to things which could be cooked in a Dutch oven or over a fire — bread pudding, or pralines. To this day, New Orleans has a lot of bakeries, turning out delicious bread and desserts.

Out in the country and in the swamps, where the Cajuns lived, things were necessarily different. The oven was often outside, and sometimes several families would bake together in one oven. In any case, Cajun likings in desserts tended to things made from leftovers and staples, bread puddings, custards, and cakes, which were easily baked right after the bread, as the oven very slowly cooled. The long baking times and lower temperatures called for reflect those times.

Glossary

A la Creole	Creole-style dishes, usually with tomatoes, green peppers, and onions.
Andouille	Hard, smoked Cajun sausage.
Bisque	Thick soup or puree made using shellfish or certain meats, served over rice.
Boudin	Cajun pork blood and rice sausage, hickory seasoned. The proportion of blood to rice makes it "white" or "red" boudin.
Cafe au lait	½ hot coffee (Louisiana dark roast or chickory) and ½ hot milk. Poured from separate containers into the cup at the same time.
Chickory	Endive. The root of the chickory is used as a substitute or adulterant in coffee. Dried, ground and added to coffee for Louisiana chickory coffee.
Cafe Noir	Black coffee.
Courtboullion	(coo bee yon) An aromatic broth in which fish has been cooked. Louisiana or Creole "coobeeyon" is a fish stew.
Crawfish	A small freshwater crustacean which looks something like a small lobster.
Creole Cuisine	A mixture of French and Spanish cooking with undertones of African American and American Indian cultures.
Daube	A round roast, usually beef, braised in stock with different seasonings and vegetables.
Daube Glacé	A roast braised with various seasonings and the addition of gelatinous substances, then refrigerated in the stock to form a cold jellied meat.
En Papillote	Baked in an oiled paper bag.
Étouffée	Shellfish, poultry or meat smothered in a covered pan with butter, cooking oil, or grease.
Filé	Powdered leaves of sassafras tree. It is sprinkled sparingly over gumbo as a flavoring and thickening agent. Never used in okra gumbo.
Flambé	Served with ignited spirits poured over.
Grillades	Beef or veal round steak, browned and then simmered until tender in a brown tomato sauce.
Jambalaya	A dish in which rice is simmered in a seasoned liquid with cooked meat, shrimp, or sausage until the liquid is absorbed by the rice. The variations are endless.
Mirliton	Also known as vegetable pear, mango squash, or chayote.
Praline	A candy patty of creamy sugar (most often brown) and pecans. Often used as a light dessert.
Gumbo	A rich soup thickened with okra or filé, containing vegetables with meat or seafood.
Remoulade	Tangy sauce of vinegar, oil, creole mustard, horseradish, and other seasonings. Served over shrimp.
Roux	An equal mixture of oil or grease and flour, browned together. Used for thickening sauces and soups.
Shallots	In Louisiana cooking, this means green onions.

Please send: 100 REX DRIVE • RIVER RIDGE, LA 70123

_____ copies of **Cooking New Orleans Style** @ $6.95 each $ _____

_____ copies of **La Bonne Cuisine** @ $11.95 each _____

_____ copies of **LBC Lagniappe** @ $3.50 each _____

Total for Books $ _____

POSTAGE AND HANDLING	Sales Tax (La. residents 4%) _____

For **Cooking New Orleans Style** or
La Bonne Cuisine:

Postage and Handling _____

1 Book only . . . . Add $2.50
2 or more to same address, shipping is free.

☐ Payment Enclosed GRAND TOTAL $ _____

Make check or money order payable to **La Bonne Cuisine**

For 1-5 **Lagniappe** books . . . . . . Add $1.00
6 or more to same address, shipping is free.

Use your VISA or MASTERCARD to order by telephone…

Order **Lagniappe** with **La Bonne Cuisine**
or **Cooking New Orleans Style**
and add no shipping for **Lagniappe!**

Charge to: **504-737-1416 or Fax 504-738-7829**

☐ VISA
☐ MASTERCARD Acct. No. _____

Exp.
Date _____ Signature _____

SEND TO: Name _____

Daytime Phone
(In Case of Problem) (_____) _____

Address _____

City/State/Zip _____

Please send: 100 REX DRIVE • RIVER RIDGE, LA 70123

_____ copies of **Cooking New Orleans Style** @ $6.95 each $ _____

_____ copies of **La Bonne Cuisine** @ $11.95 each _____

_____ copies of **LBC Lagniappe** @ $3.50 each _____

Total for Books $ _____

POSTAGE AND HANDLING	Sales Tax (La. residents 4%) _____

For **Cooking New Orleans Style** or
La Bonne Cuisine:

Postage and Handling _____

1 Book only . . . . Add $2.50
2 or more to same address, shipping is free.

☐ Payment Enclosed GRAND TOTAL $ _____

Make check or money order payable to **La Bonne Cuisine**

For 1-5 **Lagniappe** books . . . . . . Add $1.00
6 or more to same address, shipping is free.

Use your VISA or MASTERCARD to order by telephone…

Order **Lagniappe** with **La Bonne Cuisine**
or **Cooking New Orleans Style**
and add no shipping for **Lagniappe!**

Charge to: **504-737-1416 or Fax 504-738-7829**

☐ VISA
☐ MASTERCARD Acct. No. _____

Exp.
Date _____ Signature _____

Daytime Phone
(In Case of Problem) (_____) _____

SEND TO: Name _____

Address _____

City/State/Zip _____

Names and addresses of bookstores, gift shops, etc., in your area would be appreciated.

_____

_____

_____

_____

_____

_____

_____

_____

_____

_____

_____

_____

Names and addresses of bookstores, gift shops, etc., in your area would be appreciated.

_____

_____

_____

_____

_____

_____

_____

_____

_____

_____

_____

_____

_____

Please send: 100 REX DRIVE · RIVER RIDGE, LA 70123

_____ copies of **Cooking New Orleans Style**   @ $6.95 each $ _____

_____ copies of **La Bonne Cuisine**   @ $11.95 each   _____

_____ copies of **LBC Lagniappe**   @ $3.50 each   _____

                                         Total for Books $ _____

POSTAGE AND HANDLING

Sales Tax (La. residents 4%)   _____

For Cooking New Orleans Style or
La Bonne Cuisine:
1 Book only . . . . Add $2.50
2 or more to same address, shipping is free.

For 1-5 **Lagniappe** books . . . . . . Add $1.00
6 or more to same address, shipping is free.

Order **Lagniappe** with **La Bonne Cuisine**
or **Cooking New Orleans Style**
and add no shipping for **Lagniappe!**

Postage and Handling   _____

☐ Payment
   Enclosed   GRAND TOTAL $ _____

Make check or money order payable to **La Bonne Cuisine**

Use your VISA or MASTERCARD to order by telephone...

Charge to: **504-737-1416   or   Fax 504-738-7829**
☐ VISA
☐ MASTERCARD   Acct. No. _____
Exp.
Date _____ Signature _____

                                    Daytime Phone
SEND TO: Name _____   (In Case of Problem) (_____) _____

        Address _____

        City/State/Zip _____

Please send: 100 REX DRIVE · RIVER RIDGE, LA 70123

_____ copies of **Cooking New Orleans Style**   @ $6.95 each $ _____

_____ copies of **La Bonne Cuisine**   @ $11.95 each   _____

_____ copies of **LBC Lagniappe**   @ $3.50 each   _____

                                         Total for Books $ _____

POSTAGE AND HANDLING

Sales Tax (La. residents 4%)   _____

For Cooking New Orleans Style or
La Bonne Cuisine:
1 Book only . . . . Add $2.50
2 or more to same address, shipping is free.

For 1-5 **Lagniappe** books . . . . . . Add $1.00
6 or more to same address, shipping is free.

Order **Lagniappe** with **La Bonne Cuisine**
or **Cooking New Orleans Style**
and add no shipping for **Lagniappe!**

Postage and Handling   _____

☐ Payment
   Enclosed   GRAND TOTAL $ _____

Make check or money order payable to **La Bonne Cuisine**

Use your VISA or MASTERCARD to order by telephone...

Charge to: **504-737-1416   or   Fax 504-738-7829**
☐ VISA
☐ MASTERCARD   Acct. No. _____
Exp.
Date _____ Signature _____

                                    Daytime Phone
SEND TO: Name _____   (In Case of Problem) (_____) _____

        Address _____

        City/State/Zip _____

Names and addresses of bookstores, gift shops, etc., in your area would be appreciated.

_____
_____
_____
_____
_____
_____
_____
_____
_____
_____
_____

Names and addresses of bookstores, gift shops, etc., in your area would be appreciated.

_____
_____
_____
_____
_____
_____
_____
_____
_____
_____
_____